Beyond Standards

Excellence in the High School English Classroom

Carol Jago

Boynton/Cook Publishers
HEINEMANN
Portsmouth, NH

Boynton/Cook Publishers, Inc.
A subsidiary of Reed Elsevier Inc.
361 Hanover Street
Portsmouth, NH 03801-3912
www.boyntoncook.com

Offices and agents throughout the world

The author and publisher wish to thank those who have generously given permission to reprint borrowed material:

"Helping Seniors Kick In, Not Kick Back" by Carol Jago first appeared in *The Los Angeles Times*, March 23, 2000. Reprinted by permission.

Library of Congress Cataloging-in-Publication Data
Jago, Carol, 1951–
    Beyond standards : excellence in the high school English classroom / Carol Jago.
        p. cm.
    Includes bibliographic references.
    ISBN 0-86709-503-2
        1. English language—Study and teaching (Secondary)—United States.
    2. Academic achievement—United States. 3. Education—Standards—United States.   I. Title.

LB1631 .J35 2001
428'.0071'273—dc21

                                                                    00-064148

Editor: Lisa Luedeke
Production: Elizabeth Valway
Cover design: Catherine Hawkes, Cat and Mouse
Cover photo: Mike Powell/Allsport
Manufacturing: Louise Richardson

Printed in the United States of America on acid-free paper
05 04 03 02 01 DA 1 2 3 4 5

Beyond Standards

And he, who servilely creeps after sense,
Is safe, but ne'er will reach an excellence.

— John Dryden,
Tyrannic Love (1669) prologue

Contents

Foreword..ix

Introduction Standards Versus Excellence.....................................xiii

One   Engaging Reluctant Scholars.......................................1

Two   Creating the Culture of Excellence.........................16

Three   Beyond Reading Standards 28

Four   Beyond Writing Standards 42

Five   Beyond Research Standards....................................55

Six   Beyond Literature Standards..................................69

Seven   Beyond Assessment Standards 88

Eight   Beyond Teaching Standards....................................97

Works Cited 104

To my students, who never stop teaching me.

Foreword

I have known Carol Jago for about thirty years, and I regard her as not only one of the finest teachers I have ever encountered, but one of the memorably great teachers of her generation. Thousands of Santa Monica High School students would agree. Many of them would be able to add stories about how Carol's instruction changed their lives, inspired them as readers and ethical persons, and led them to universities and productive careers that they might never have aspired to or qualified for without the challenges she set for them and the demands she helped them meet. Although she was never my teacher (I was, in fact, hers), Carol has taught me a great deal over the years, just as she has taught large numbers of her colleagues through her work as the director of the California Reading and Literature Project at UCLA (CRLP), her many essays published in teachers' professional journals, her leadership role in the National Council of Teachers of English (NCTE), and her work as the longtime editor of *California English*, the quarterly of the California Association of Teachers of English (CATE).

Carol has recently taken on the larger challenge of writing entire books about her teaching. The first three were published within a year of one another. All of them are on teaching literature, and demonstrate Carol's expertise as a classroom practitioner and the catholicity of her literary taste. Her first book, *Nikki Giovanni in the Classroom* (NCTE, 1999), is on teaching that poet's works, her second, *With Rigor for All* (Calendar Islands, 2000), is on teaching the literary classics to today's high school students. Her third book, *Alice Walker in the Classroom* (NCTE, 2000), is a handy guide for bringing this celebrated author's work into the classroom. Aside from having value as contributions to our professional knowledge about the teaching of literature, these books enhance Carol's reputation as a professional phenomenon: She wrote them while continuing to teach, direct CRLP, edit *California English*, write a regular column on education for the *Los Angeles Times*, contribute to NCTE—and spend quality time with her husband and teenage son.

With this her fourth book, Carol Jago confirms her place among a select group of classroom teachers whose writing has transformed professional discourse and the teaching of English in our time. I'm thinking about such practitioners as Regie Routman, Linda Rief, Jeff Wilhelm, Nancie Atwell, and Tom Romano, all of whom have used their extensive teaching experience and samples of student talk and writing to open up their classrooms to professional scrutiny and to share their goals, methods, and reflections with their colleagues.

Beyond Standards, like the books of all these teacher-writers, has a particularly powerful persuasive force by virtue of the richness of detail drawn from Carol Jago's high school classes. Her accounts and analyses of what transpires in her classroom constitute what the anthropologist Clifford Geertz, borrowing a term from Gilbert Ryle, calls a "thick description," an account of life in a particular cultural situation that includes rich details that give the account verisimilitude for the reader.

But Carol's book doesn't simply reveal the life in her classroom. It also advances an argument and defends a particular approach to teaching and learning high school English. Her argument is at once an endorsement and a critique of the current emphasis on using standards for teaching and for assessing learning in English-language arts. At a moment in educational history when standards are being sold to voters, the press, and boards of education as the latest panacea for the imagined failures of public education, Carol endorses standards, but only to the extent that they set useful and challenging goals for students. More often, she criticizes particular standards and the standards movement for setting unworthy and trivial goals compared to the goals that students and teachers will set for themselves—and achieve—when they are engaged in the serious and satisfying work of authentic reading, writing, and language study.

This book may be seen as a series of stories or ethnographic studies on how to make the work of the high school English class genuinely important to students, so that they will engage in literary activity with the kind of attention to and investment in the outcome of their work that is characteristic of writers and readers who are engaged in intellectual work in the real world. Carol presents generous samples of student talk and writing to demonstrate that, given the right conditions, students will learn more—and produce more useful and impressive products—than any standards document could possibly anticipate.

Carol's book is also punctuated throughout with the kind of practical wisdom and good-humored cantankerousness that a teacher develops by spending twenty-five or thirty years in the classroom devoted to teaching—ultimately more interested in what happens in the minds and hearts of her students than her lesson plan and syllabus. Speaking for all her colleagues, Carol calls legislators, school boards, administrators, and the fickle public to task for the disrespect and ignorance they show for the work of teaching, when they propose to evaluate teachers on the basis of test scores (which can measure only trivial accomplishments) at the same time that they fail to provide the conditions that are required for optimal teaching and learning—conditions like clean and safe schools, books for every student, planning time for teachers, and instructional periods that are protected from interruptions.

Carol is also refreshingly candid about her own failures with some students and about the educational community's responsibility for the failures of entire groups of students. And she is equally candid in her analysis of what it will take to correct those failures.

What may be most refreshing about this book for many readers is the voice that informs it—the personality and wit that Carol's friends and colleagues so appreciate. Those who know Carol Jago personally know that she is one of the world's great readers. I do not believe I have ever met anyone who reads more widely or more voraciously than Carol does. She reads (and rereads) classic, modern, and experimental literature; every recent Nobel Prize winner and Pulitzer Prize winner; literary and social criticism; books about education; biographies; the work of established and emerging poets; everything that is written about schools; and virtually every book published for the young adult audience.

Several of the most important books I read over the past decade or more were recommended to me by Carol; in some cases, they were given to me by Carol—not lent, but given. She is famous for becoming so enthusiastic about a book that she buys extra copies to give to her friends and students. A similar generosity is evident throughout *Beyond Standards*, in which Carol has a book or poem to recommend for every teaching situation and every level of student ability. This work is also a small treasury of quotable lines from Carol's wide reading—lines that readers will want to write down and remember.

I predict that among all the books English teachers read this year, few will be as much marked up with underlining and notes in margins and on endpages as this volume, which is packed with good thinking and helpful ideas for the practicing English teacher. Whether you are a veteran at the verge of retirement, in mid-career (even in mid-career crisis), or struggling through the early years of figuring out what and how to teach, you will find in this book the kind of philosophical perspective, psychological support, and practical advice you can get from only the wisest, most witty, and most generous of colleagues. My advice to you is to read this book and be grateful for the colleague you find in it.

Sheridan Blau
University of California
Santa Barbara, CA

Introduction
Standards Versus Excellence

Every educational pundit, every politician, has something to say about standards, and for the most part they all say the same thing: "We love 'em!" What I believe is shortsighted about the national race to standards-based education is that when we identify exactly what students should know and be able to do, we inadvertently create a ceiling for achievement. Extraordinary performance and true excellence in writing or thinking never appear on the charts. Even extraordinarily rigorous documents like the California and Massachusetts language arts standards don't deal with excellence. Why? Because excellence can't be prescribed.

It would be unfair to create standards that only a few could ever achieve—and those few only when the wind of inspiration was blowing in the right direction. Such standards would go against the spirit and purpose of the standards movement, a movement fueled by the genuine desire to improve student achievement. Call me a naive idealist, but I wouldn't stay in the classroom if I didn't believe that, given knowledgeable teachers, adequate textbooks, and clean and safe schools, most children can achieve at the academic level that is now law. What I worry about is that, in the process of putting standards into practice to raise the level of student performance, we might also limit or circumscribe that performance.

The standards movement has been a wonderful vehicle for conversations about curriculum and instruction. As Linda Darling-Hammond, William F. Russell Professor of Education and codirector of the National Center for Restructuring Education, Schools, and Teaching at Teachers College, Columbia University, explains (1997):

The fundamental premise of today's standards-based reform is that challenging education goals and contemporary knowledge about how people learn can be incorporated into practice when standards guide decisions about curriculum, teaching, and assessment. The power of standards as tools for guiding practice can be seen in other countries' schools and in the professions that have built a strong knowledge base that is acknowledged as the foundation for professional decisions. (212)

I am convinced that children will benefit from the focused attention the standards movement has brought to student learning. What concerns me is that some of our children can do much, much more than any standards document describes. We need to make sure that in our push to achieve standards, we don't forget about inspiring excellence.

What do I mean by *excellence*? I recall classroom discussions about *Crime and Punishment* so powerful that I could only stand back and listen and learn. I have read student essays so original that putting a grade on the paper seemed an insult to the writer. I think of a poem by twelfth grader Kelsey Walker:

In This Language

In this language, there are no nevers,
No can'ts, no won'ts, no shouldn'ts,
Only chances, dreams, and endless beginnings.
The logical can hardly speak it.
In this language no pain, only joy.
Your heart swells, emotions building up inside of you
Like water pushing at a dam.
Sick people are never left for dead.
Tears are never shed in desperation.
Something inside whispers to you in this language while
    you sleep.
Faces in the crowd speak only kind words.
Old ladies put away quilts and blankets,
Bring out the white shoes and start spring cleaning.
In this language you can never give up,

You can't say "No."
Once a sentence starts it is filled with hope
And grief and failures melt away.
Inflections like birdsong lilt in the sunshine
Softening harsh words until they are filled with life.

Outstanding student work doesn't just happen. It requires support and thrives in particular classroom climates. Almost always it appears effortless. Behind Kelsey's seeming ease with words are the dozens of books of poetry she read over the course of the semester and the hundreds of poems she has written since she was a child. My challenge as a teacher is to find ways to help other students become as passionate about learning something—about learning anything—as Kelsey is about poetry.

I never tell students that learning will be proof against bad times or troubles, only that the habit of learning is a powerful antidote to despair. Too often we make false promises to students about the benefits of a good education, lining up any number of goodies that await them at the finish line: entrance to prestigious colleges, high-paying jobs, financial security. In fact, the race only begins at graduation. The truth is that students who have had an excellent education know how to learn—and, on occasion, take pleasure in learning.

Of course a teacher often needs wizard-like skills to make this happen in the real world of public education. I teach English in a comprehensive high school and have 169 students enrolled in my five classes. Each of these classes requires a different preparation. Of my students, one-fourth speak a language other than English at home: Spanish, Korean, Farsi, Mandarin, Hebrew, or Russian. Some are perfectly fluent in English; others still struggle. Twenty-three percent of the school's 3,200 students qualify for the free or reduced-price meals program. We also teach the children of movie stars and university professors. Almost all teachers on the faculty have sent, are sending, or plan to send their children to the school.

Santa Monica High School is a wonderful, frustrating, crazy place. Some days I can't believe I made it to the last bell without screaming. On others I drive home in a dream, fully aware of how lucky I am to have landed in such rich soil.

The kind of work I want from my students goes beyond any list of standards, skills to be mastered, or even books to be read. It has to do with habits of mind, thoughtfulness, and personal integrity toward intellectual pursuits that I find hard to prescribe but have, on occasion, been able to inspire. In the pages that follow, I have tried to show you what this looks like. Welcome to my classroom, E200.

Beyond Standards

One

Engaging Reluctant Scholars

*M*y period five students enter the classroom with their mouths still full from lunch. Oscar arrives with a pizza box that attracts Jessica from the other side of the room. Cristina comes in laden with three bouquets of flowers and six helium birthday balloons. Matt and Ryan are roughhousing near the computers, but before I can tell them to watch out for the monitors, the bell rings. Not one of the thirty-six students in attendance pays a bit of mind. In case you were wondering, this isn't a third-grade classroom but twelfth-grade English, and my plan for the day is the study of Quincy Troupe's poetry. Employing every classroom management skill I know (and a few I invented over lunch), I bring these pulsing teenagers to relative order.

My students don't mean to make teaching difficult. They simply have 1,001 more important things on their minds than the lesson at hand. Or so they believe. My challenge is to create a bridge between a few of those 1,001 things and their class work. I use the word *work* here intentionally. Teachers err when we tell students that "learning is fun," though not because it can't be. The mistake is in placing learning in competition with pizza, flowers, and balloons. Lunch beats senior English every time. I know these students are capable of excellence, but it takes more than cheerleading on my part to help them achieve. It takes work.

Another Kind of PE—Poetic Education

Mens sana in corpore sano, "a sound mind in a sound body," has long been the motto of educators keen to nurture children. As a result, most states mandate participation in physical education classes. I would like to suggest another kind of PE that is equally important for a child's well-being: *poetic education.* Unless children exercise regularly with words, many will never develop the imaginative muscles they need to survive in the troublesome workaday world. A good poem can make getting up in the morning bearable. Occasionally a poem may win over the person you love. Some poems offer solace more lasting than Prozac.

While most states' standards documents make reference to the study of poetry as an important and lasting part of a high school education, none that I have seen include the writing of poetry. While hardly a workplace skill, writing poetry is, to my mind and in my experience with typically troubled teens, a survival skill. Student poetry is difficult to assess, but when excellent poems are shared in class, everyone knows it: A for applause.

Just as PE coaches demand that students, whatever their natural talent, get out there and move, effective poetic education teachers demand that students write. Working as I do with twelfth graders coming to the end of their high school years, I like to ask students to look back and consider where they have been, as well as where they are going. I asked one class to take out a sheet of paper, fold it down the middle, and on the left side make a list of all the things they remembered doing as a child. As they wrote, I interrupted them with suggestions: "Think about the games you used to play, your favorite flavored popsicle, your favorite toys. Who was important to you then? Where did you like to hide? What were you afraid of?"

When most had filled the column, I asked them to move to the right-hand side of the page and make a list of the things they did today, the foods they ate now, the places they hung out, their favorite teenage toys. I then handed out copies of Quincy Troupe's "Flying Kites," a two-stanza poem in which Troupe makes a comparison between flying kites as a child and flying words as an adult poet. After talking about the poem, I invited students to borrow the first words of Troupe's two stanzas, "We used to" and "Now we," and write poems of their own exploring these two worlds. Jason Speciner, an accomplished discus thrower, wrote:

> We used to have a bedtime
> Sleep was mandatory,
> Strictly enforced by parents looking for order
> It was important
> A long night's rest was needed
> To prepare for another long day.
> Today we have no curfew
> Sleep is secondary
> Night time becomes the playground
> Parents need not apply
> Now a long day's rest is needed
> Needed for another long night.

I believe this kind of exercise with words helps students make sense of how their lives are changing. Writing poetry forces them to stop and take stock. What was it like to be a child? What is it like to be almost grown?

Over half the class used the assignment to compare their relationships with the opposite sex then and now. Oscar Perez wasn't thinking about standards or excellence when he wrote the following poem, but he certainly achieved beyond what I had expected from such a simple assignment.

> We used to chase girls across the school
> Teachers shouting for us to stop
> Playing spin the bottle
> Making every girl blush.
> Now we get chased by girls

3

Our parents telling us to be careful
Phones ringing, pagers vibrating, e-mails coming
Making us blush.

A few students, like Nancy Carrasco, reflected on how their relationships with important adults in their lives had changed over time.

We used to go to grandma's every day
Listening to her stories, eating her fabulous food
That would fill our tummies
Now we ignore that once-loved grandma
Because she screams at us for
Our hair, our tattoos, our piercings.

Teaching seniors during the last few weeks before graduation can be a challenge. Utterly distracted by plans for prom and dreams of summer, seventeen-year-olds revert in the homestretch to their most childish selves. One locks the keys inside his car—with the radio playing. Another asks me if it would be all right if he went home to swim instead of coming to class. They look at me as though I have two heads for suggesting that waltzing in five minutes late is a problem. Once dutiful, they now reside in a zone of their own.

In an effort to maintain my own sanity as well as a semblance of instruction, I decided to craft a series of lessons focusing on the transition from childhood to adulthood. My guess was that some of the outlandish behavior my students exibited was a response to their fear about what lay ahead. I began with a poem by Portia Nelson, called "Autobiography in Five Short Chapters," in which Nelson describes the narrator's developing relationship with a hole in the ground. First she falls straight in without ever noticing it. Then she sees the hole but still takes a tumble. Finally she takes responsibility for walking around the ubiquitous hole (sincere apologies for this paraphrase of Nelson's elegant lines). I asked students to write a poem, modeled after Nelson's, describing in the first four stanzas some aspect of their experience of high school from freshman to senior year. The fifth stanza was to depict the future.

Within twenty minutes these seemingly disaffected young people had written some of the most powerful poetry I had read all semester. Chris charted the progress of his party going. Rakefet recalled auditioning for her first play. Luchino outlined his locker room development from tormented to tormentor. Debbie described hiding in her desk and how the once invisible monsters became manageable (though they never quite went away).

Michael Hibbert wrote about his own need for escape from the confines of high school. He read an early draft of this poem to the class; other students liked it so much that I asked Mike if he would mind if we used the draft as a model for revision. He was keen to get specific feedback and readily agreed. I first asked the class to identify the lines they liked best and to tell Mike what it was that made those particular words sing for them. I then asked Mike if he thought there were any places where the poem fell flat. He identified a few and asked for suggestions. We didn't "fix" Mike's poem for him, but helped him see how he could make it better. The following poem is a good example of a student going far beyond standards to excellence.

Chapter 1
I enter the cage
All around me are the flutterings of wings
Like fireworks
Where I belong, where I go
Found a little spot
Found a little friend
As I sat with the sparrows
Talking games

Chapter 2
I hang on fences with crows
Dressed in black, singing songs
Hung with bats, upside down
With nowhere to go but
Down

Chapter 3
I found a cool perch
Where the parrots like to be
They were loud and beautiful
But mostly they were loud

Chapter 4
I strutted down the sidewalk
With the pigeons going coo coo coo coo
A bunch of city birds with nowhere to go
We always end up almost
Getting run over by cars

Chapter 5
Angels
Over in the corner
That I didn't see before
That nobody saw
The cage is too small, too dark, too loud
Too dangerous
We are Lost Angels
Watch
We fly away.

I may be reading into this poem something that isn't there, but the image of "lost angels" in the final paragraph had particular resonance for me given that we live in a city called Los Angeles. Senioritis or no, it seemed a very good day's work.

Do such lessons prepare students for college? After graduation, Mike went off to university, where in the fall quarter he wrote a novel. I look forward to his first book of poetry. *Mens sana in corpore sano*. As we design curriculum with excellence in mind, let's not forget our students' poetic education.

What Is a Standard, *Anyway?*

According to the *Oxford English Dictionary*, a *standard* is a "flag, sculptured figure, or other conspicuous object raised on a pole to indicate a rallying point." Such a vertical image is quite different from the interpretation most educators ascribe to the term *standard*. In current parlance, a standard is a horizontal bar students must clear before they can be allowed to progress to the next grade. Instead of a lofty image designed to inspire Herculean effort in the field, standards have become hurdles students must overcome. While children may not be able to articulate this difference, the symbolism is not lost on learners.

Take for example the poetry lessons I just described. Employing the model of a standard as a rallying point, I offered students models of professional, exemplary work. Together we read Quincy Troupe's and Portia Nelson's poems, and I then asked students to see if they could aim at this *standard* and create a poem of their own. The quality of their work suggests to me that students were indeed inspired by this standard, reaching beyond their usual range of expression and taking chances with self-revelation just as Troupe and Nelson had and in the process creating something quite outstanding.

A more typical standards-based approach might have been to place a copy of a standard on the board, for example, New Jersey Language Arts Literacy Standard 3.3: "All students will write in clear, concise, organized language that varies in content and form for different audiences and purposes." While certainly a noble goal, this standard is hardly one to capture the hearts and minds of seventeen-year-olds. And lest you think I exaggerate to suggest one might actually use the language of standards documents in a classroom, teachers in San Diego City Schools are currently required to display the particular standard that the day's lesson has been designed to help students achieve.

Like many dumb rules, this one was instituted for a seemingly reasonable purpose. San Diego school administrators want teachers to think about the California language arts standards as they plan curriculum. They want to remind teachers of the larger context within which any single lesson should be imbedded. What every classroom teacher knows from experience is that simply posting signs around the room—"No eating in class!" "Leave gum at the door!" "Cheaters Never Prosper!"—does little to influence student behavior. Behavior modification, whether it be a student's or a teacher's, must engage those whose behavior is to be modified on a deeper level. If standards are to rally students to achieve, they must be more than bumper stickers.

Students as Judges of Their Own Work

Another area where policymakers in education have taken a wrong turn is in assessment. In the past I have taken a rabid anti–test prep stance, believing that coursework in English should remain pure, focusing on literary analysis and development of student writing. I was sure such instruction prepared my students well for any qualifying exams they had to face. The more I came to understand standardized assessments, the more I began to see that my idealistic stance was holding some students back. With a few changes in my curriculum and without distorting what I believe about learning, I discovered ways to shape instruction that allowed students to demonstrate what they know under the artificial circumstances of multiple-choice questioning. A description of these methods can be found in Chapter Six. As I look into a crystal ball, I do not foresee a time, at least in my professional lifetime, when students will not have to sit for high-stakes tests.

Along with preparing students for the ubiquitous standardized tests, we also need to teach them to evaluate their work for themselves. What kind of learners have we created if students feel they must turn to an adult or an outside measure to determine the value of what they produce? How long would writers, musicians, or creative entrepreneurs survive if they had to check at every turn with outside evaluators to ensure that their work was worthy of continued effort? Children need to learn how to spot excellence for themselves.

As my students worked their way through the Quincy Troupe poetry lesson, I interrupted them to ask if anyone had a promising draft to share. Never one to leave a classroom moment like this to chance, I had queried a few of the students I assisted during the work period to see if they would be willing to read what they had written thus far. They almost all said yes. Before the writers began to read, I assigned a designated listener. Students understand the responsibilities entailed in such a role from their drivers' education classes. Like a designated driver, a designated listener must be totally alert as the work is read and be prepared to offer specific comments about lines, phrases, or ideas that are particularly effective. As Joseph Addison wrote in the *Spectator* (1712), "A true critic ought to dwell rather upon excellencies than imperfections, to discover the concealed beauties of a writer, and communicate to the world such things as are worth their observation."

After Nancy Carasco read the poem about her grandmother's criticism of piercings and tattoos, Jenny Menedez— Nancy's designated listener—responded,

> This is so true. My mother had me change my clothes three times before we went to visit my grandma last Sunday. What was really good was the way you seemed sorry that the good times when your grandmother liked you exactly as you were and fed you delicious food are gone forever. I feel this really powerful thing in your poem, Nancy, though I'm not sure exactly what words made me feel it, that you are also saying you aren't going to take out the rings for her, no matter what your grandma thinks or how much you love her.

What I am trying to accomplish with designated listeners is to get past the "I liked it a lot" responses and help students practice identifying exactly what is excellent in their classmates' work. The first step is to identify these qualities in someone else's poem; the second is to identify them in their own work. From the sidelines, I sometimes offer suggestions: "Did you notice how Jason's clever reversal of the line 'A long night's rest was needed / To prepare for another long day' to 'Now a long day's rest is needed / Needed for another long night' made all of us smile? Why did you grin at that, Cesar?" I never feel guilty about putting students on the spot with a question like this one—I saw the smile on Cesar's lips. Trying to articulate what is excellent about Jason's poem will help Cesar begin to understand how lines on a page affect a reader.

Cesar wasn't a bit put off. "Um, well, I mean like Jason's poem puts it out there about how we all stay out really late and our parents are always mad, but we do it anyway. I bet you just called on me because I was sleeping in class yesterday, Mrs. Jago."

"Astute observation, Mr. De la Torre. What else was there about the contrast between Jason's two lines that you liked?"

"I guess it makes me think of being tucked in at night by my mom and how good that felt, and now how bad it feels to be so tired all day because I stayed out so late. There's a kind of balance between these two lines like they're on opposite sides of a teeter-totter. One goes up. The other comes down."

I hope that identifying the exemplary elements in sample student poems will also help those who are stuck get started. Too often teenagers give up before they actually begin. After a lively discussion of drafts that show hints of technical prowess or particular personal honesty, a few students who were temporarily satisfied with a shabby piece of writing sometimes crumple up what they have done and start again. There is no need for an ugly red stamped "REDO" on their drafts. These students see for themselves that they can do much better a second time around.

Grades That Matter

Just as standardized assessments can work against students developing internal performance standards, so can grades. In his now classic text *Punished by Rewards* (1993), Alfie Kohn offers a powerful argument against using grades or other rewards to motivate students:

> Grades cannot be justified on the grounds that they motivate students, because they actually undermine the sort of motivation that leads to excellence. Using them to sort students undercuts our efforts to educate. And to the extent we want to offer students feedback about their performance—a goal that demands a certain amount of caution lest their involvement in the task itself be sacrificed—there are better ways to do this than by giving grades. (203)

I believe that if an assignment is carefully structured, grades can actually become superfluous.

As the final copies of student "We used to / Now we" poems began finding their way to my desk, I knew that simply assigning grades to this work would not be enough. We needed to celebrate this writing. As soon as the bell rang to begin class, I announced that we would be publishing these poems in an anthology. Turning to the shyest and most thoughtful student in the room, I asked Michelle if she would agree to be our editor. Having no idea what this might entail, she agreed. I then passed back all the poems that had been turned in, saying that if we planned to publish them, every one of the poems needed to be reread and checked for spelling and mechanical errors. I went to the computer and quickly created a form that read, "I hereby stake my reputation as a student and a writer on the technical correctness of this poem." Below the statement were lines for three signatures. No one could submit a poem to Michelle before three other students had read it.

As students worked on one another's poems, I noticed that they behaved more like comrades than error police. There was a shared purpose for this good behavior—a publication in which we all could take pride. Making it up as I went along, I told students that the anthology would be distributed at local bookstores and public libraries and that we would sell any extras we had to other students for a dollar. (I always think it is better to charge a token amount for something than to give it away. Somehow, putting a price on a publication makes it seem more valuable.) Nancy had the excellent idea to send copies to Quincy Troupe and Portia Nelson. I sent her to a computer to see if she could find Internet addresses or contact numbers for them.

As pages began accumulating on Michelle's desk, I suggested that she begin thinking about grouping the poems by theme and considering which poems might be best to appear first and last in the collection. When William handed in his poem, I asked if he would mind designing a cover for us. I had noticed he was always doodling and thought he might like to try his hand at a public picture. I told him to make sure to sign his design. Once the cover was complete, we voted on a color. I wrote a short introduction explaining the assignment and thanking Quincy Troupe and Portia Nelson for inspiring such extraordinary student work. Piece by piece, our booklet came together.

When copies arrived from the print shop a week later, you would have thought I was handing out prizes. Students were thrilled to see their poems in print and bound with care. One group of girls asked for an extra copy to bring to their last year's ESL teacher to show her how well they were doing in a regular English class. They signed their names below their poems. I can't imagine that a grade of A on any single piece of paper would have made them nearly this happy. Those students who, through procrastination, absence, or misadventure, didn't have their poems in the anthology were truly dismayed; much more so, I think, than they would have been with a zero in my grade book.

We weren't through, though. I wanted students to look again and judge what they and their classmates had done in terms of excellence. I took a large envelope and labeled it "Mailbox." I told students that after they read through the anthology, they should write three letters to classmates whose poems had affected them powerfully, explaining as well as they could why this was and what in the poem was so powerful. Though I promised not to read what they wrote, all letters had to be signed.

At the end of class, I distributed the mail. Suddenly it was absolutely clear whose poems had had the deepest impact upon readers. This didn't feel like a competition or popularity contest, but rather a simple and straightforward acknowledgment of the poems that truly were the best in our collection. Yasmin Sandoval's desk was showered with notes. Here is the poem that inspired her classmates' overwhelming response:

What We Used to Do

We used to think we would never grow up
Hiding in the bathroom
Turning off the lights and calling on *La Llorona*
Running out screaming
Becoming the characters from last night's novela
Fighting off boys with cooties because you didn't want to be
Sitting in a tree K-I-S-S-I-N-G
We raced to get to the *paletero*
To buy *chicharrones* with lemon and *chile*
Making our lips red as the lipstick we'd steal
From our mom when we played house
We couldn't wait until the next day
To talk about things, girl-talk
Making sure to pinky swear or hope to die.

Now we are older
And write notes to keep in touch
Talk on the phone and make our moms mad about the bill
Gossip about who's in love but isn't loved
Who is loved but doesn't want that love
Making plans for the weekend
Forgetting our problems
Forgetting that we are broken-hearted
Eating, dancing, laughing, taking pictures

Knowing that tomorrow
Everything we do now
Will only be
What we used to do.

As you might have guessed from my opening description of this group of students, many of them do not worry much about their grades. For some a C is just fine and even a D is acceptable given that it still carries credit toward graduation. Motivating such students to work toward excellence is a challenge. I need a standard that will rally me, their teacher, as well as one for my talented but reluctant scholars. Poems like Yasmin's have become such a standard.

One Size Fits Few

In *One Size Fits Few: The Folly of Educational Standards* (1999), Susan Ohanian argues that the standards movement has actually done damage to instruction in America. She concludes that

> America's teachers and children don't need national committees to grade their worth. We need local teachers to reflect on their own experiences, to figure out how the students, the curriculum, and even the bureaucracy interact in a process we call education. The essence of being a teacher is knowing who you are, where you are—and liking what you find. (151)

No teachers worthy of that title would like what they found if their students weren't learning. No high school English instructor could feel good about a school year if her students weren't writing better in June than they did in September. From my perspective, the biggest problem schools face is providing teachers and students with working conditions that allow them to achieve. Neither sticks nor carrots will motivate instructors and their charges to reach for higher standards nearly so much as the following will:

- Clean and safe schools in which to work.
- Classes of no more than twenty students.
- Books for every student.
- Planning time for every teacher.
- Instructional time that is held sacred. No interruptions!

Under such conditions, I might be able to do the job I know I am capable of. Threatening teachers with docked pay or decreased funding for their schools if students do not meet standardized testing targets is a foolish way to motivate professionals. Promise me I can have everything on this list, and I promise you my students will learn.

Two

Creating the Culture of Excellence

"*A* woeful putrefaction threatens the Rising Generation; barbarous Ignorance, and the unavoidable consequence of it, Outrageous Wickedness will make the Rising Generation Loathsome, if it have not Schools to preserve it." Does the warning sound a familiar note? In fact, Cotton Mather wrote this sentence two hundred years ago describing Puritan teenagers in rural New England. And he had never heard a single lyric of gangsta rap.

Mather's solution to the problem of young people's natural tendency toward waywardness was education. He wrote that, "A Good School deserves to be call'd the very Salt of the Town that hath it." I agree. Without a school "wherein the Youth may by able Masters be Taught the Things that are necessary to qualify them for future Serviceableness, and have their Manners therewithal well-formed under a Laudable Discipline," a community will founder. Unless we can discover ways to do more than simply house students in classrooms for seventeen years and actually inspire young people to excellence, we are going to be spending a great deal of time lamenting their lack of "serviceableness."

Able Masters as Models of Excellence

How is it possible to create schools that function as the "salt" of sprawling metropolises like Los Angeles, Chicago, and New York? First, we need *able masters*—teachers with a love and deep knowledge of their subject matter who can awaken the same in students. This may mean bringing into the profession poets, mathematicians, musicians, engineers, and scientists who have not passed through formal education programs. It may also mean paying them extra for their expertise or bringing them in part time to teach a class or two on campus. Such suggestions give teachers unions the jitters, but schools are going to have to look outside traditional pathways for more able masters to provide models of excellence that students can aspire to.

Whenever I have had poets from the Poets in the Schools project or writers from PEN in the Classroom come to visit and work with my students, instruction comes alive. There is something about meeting someone who actually does for a living what is being studied that focuses students' attention. Questions leap from their lips: So how did you first send out your work? Do you really need an agent? How much did you get paid for that? Someone always asks Where do you get your ideas?

Along with able masters from outside the classroom, we need to ensure that there are able masters within. The California State University-Long Beach issues a warranty for each of its seven hundred graduating student teachers. Under a policy adopted in 1999 and praised by Charles B. Reed, chancellor of the California State University system, the university guarantees the job performance of its novice teachers. But unlike dysfunctional toasters, newly hired teachers cannot be returned for replacement. The university promises to send out education professors to assist any floundering teachers.

On the surface this is a wonderful idea. The first year of teaching is enormously challenging whatever your preparation has been, and, without support, many talented new teachers simply throw up their hands and walk away. Thirty percent quit within the first five years. As for warranties, I just don't think novice teachers have much in common with household appliances. And a guarantee from a university that is busy training next year's seven hundred graduates seems improbable. Such a program garners headlines but is unlikely to solve real problems. The place to support new teachers is in the schools. Moreover, the people who need to be providing that support are the novice's new colleagues. If we are serious about providing every child with an able master, every new teacher needs a site buddy as a mentor.

Languishing Under Discouragements

Later in his essay, Cotton Mather writes that "the Devil cannot give a greater Blow to the Reformation among us, than by causing Schools to Languish under Discouragements." Unfortunately, that is exactly what happens at all too many schools. How, for example, is it possible for a teacher who is intent upon holding her students to high standards of excellence to carry on when she has no books? The ablest masters in the world can't teach *The Grapes of Wrath* with only a classroom set of books that students aren't allowed to take home. Discouraged, teachers stop assigning long novels and curricular excellence suffers.

In 1997 education writer Amy Pyle made the front page of the *Los Angeles Times* with her exposé of textbook shortages in California classrooms. She reported 54 percent of California teachers said they did not have enough books to allow students to take copies home; 24 percent reported that their students didn't even have books in class. This bad news met with universal outrage and hand-over-heart promises that "matters would be looked into" and "things would change," but the shortage continues.

Next to competent teachers, nothing influences learning more than textbooks. Good ones stimulate interest. Dilapidated, out-of-date, and defaced books say to students that we don't care very much about their learning or, indeed, very much about them. One problem is that buying new textbooks lacks the sex appeal of buying new technology. While grant opportunities for computer curricula and Internet connections abound, it's almost impossible to write an appealing grant application for more copies of *The Scarlet Letter.*

Experienced teachers rarely "stick to the book," but new teachers simply don't have the resources that a publisher does in terms of models, sample assignments, and enrichment activities for students. Textbooks provide an important temporary scaffolding for their teaching.

It may seem odd to be taking guidance from a seventeenth-century Puritan, but I know I couldn't say it better: "Where schools are not vigorously and Honourably Encouraged, whole Colonies will sink apace into a Degenerate and Contemptible Condition, and at last become horribly Barbarous. If you would not betray your Posterity into the very Circumstances of Savages, let Schools have more Encouragement."

Conditions That Support Excellence

What contemporary reform-minded politicians don't seem to understand is that schools are complex communities. Some of these communities, like the one in Santa Monica where I have worked my whole professional life, are built on trust. Although teachers, parents, administrators, and students may disagree—sometimes vehemently—with one another, beneath the point of contention is the fundamental belief that everyone in the system is operating in good faith. I have never doubted that the leaders in my school community put children first.

In all too many school communities, there is little trust. Administrators keen to respond to the latest education initiative put pressure on teachers to raise academic standards. What these eager administrators often forget is that many of their teachers have been holding children to high standards for years. Looking for a quick fix, administrators don't trust the successful teachers and successful classroom practices that are already in place. Placing their trust in educational "experts," administrators often forget to ask the very people who know best—experienced teachers—how to make things better.

On their part, teachers distrust the motives of politicians who have suddenly made academic standards the flavor of the month. In his 1998 inaugural speech, California governor

Gray Davis announced that he would not run for reelection unless test scores went up. Many teachers shook their heads and yawned at such posturing, thinking, "Come visit my classroom, where there are no books and a leaky roof, before you make such promises, Governor. Count how many of my students come to school hungry." Demanding that teachers raise academic standards may garner headlines, but it only exacerbates the distrust teachers already feel toward a system that institutionally shortchanges many children.

All students need and deserve

- A caring, well-educated teacher with professional time in the day for preparing lessons, holding student conferences, making parent phone calls, and evaluating student work.
- A safe, clean environment in which to learn. Students must accept responsibility for maintaining both the safety and the cleanliness of their school.
- Up-to-date textbooks that are in good condition. Students must take responsibility for taking care of their schoolbooks and must be prepared to replace any they have damaged.
- Well-equipped science laboratories.
- Access to technology, not only during the school day but also before and after school.
- Classroom libraries and school libraries that are teeming with books for all tastes and interests.
- Athletic programs that are sometimes competitive and sometimes just for fun.
- Music, art, and dance programs run by talented adults who love working with kids.

You get the picture. Why are we surprised when children who have all or most of the things I describe do well in school while students who don't drop out? Have you ever noticed what powerful predictors school ZIP codes are of test scores?

Political candidates need to get their minds around the idea that shouting "Higher! Harder! More!" is never going to raise academic standards. What it takes is determined leadership committed to supporting schools where conditions for excellence are commonplace. I don't believe this is beyond our country's means. The question is, do we have the will?

The Power of Their Ideas

One educator who has demonstrated that she has the will is Deborah Meier. Founder of the Central Park East Schools and fellow at the Annenberg Institute for School Reform, Meier has been a tireless champion of children's right to a stimulating education (1995):

> The task of creating environments where all kids can experience the power of their ideas requires unsettling not only our accepted organization of schooling and our unspoken and unacknowledged agreement about the purposes of schools. Taking this task seriously also means calling into question our definitions of intelligence and the ways in which we judge each other. And taking it seriously means accepting public responsibility for the shared future of the next generation. It's a task for all of us, not just school people or policymakers or even parents alone. The stakes are enormous, and the answers within our reach. (4)

Teaching at Central Park East Schools revolves around the implementation of what Meier calls "habits of mind." Whatever the subject or text being scrutinized, students are taught to apply these five questions to their study:

- How do we know what we know?
- Whose perspective does this represent?
- How is this related to that?
- How might things have been otherwise?
- Why is this important?

According to Meier, it is the fifth habit-of-mind question that is the most important. "Who cares? Knowing and learning take on importance only when we are convinced it matters, it makes a difference" (41). These habits of mind also need to be practiced daily to become part of how students approach the world, as well as of how they approach a book.

I know that the most powerful learning that occurs in my classroom happens when students care about what we are reading. You might think that after teaching tenth grade for twenty-five years I would have figured out exactly which texts sixteen-year-olds find important, and would be able to offer a foolproof list of novels certain to captivate your students. Unfortunately (and fortunately), teaching isn't that tidy.

Allowing Students to Decide What Is Important

This fall my tenth graders threw me a real curveball when, after reading *Beowulf*, John Gardner's *Grendel*, and *Frankenstein*, Gabe and Claire approached me after class to ask why we couldn't read *The Hunchback of Notre Dame* next. The easy answer was that the school didn't have copies of the book, but they were persistent. "I heard it has this monster in it, and I'll bet he's a lot like Grendel and Victor Frankenstein's monster," urged Claire. Applauding her employment of the third habit-of-mind question—How is this related to that?—I was tempted to take a chance.

Gabe chimed in, "You always get to pick the books, Mrs. Jago. It should be our turn." I told them they could make their case to the class and see if others were willing to buy copies. Claire quickly checked Amazon.com and found an abridged version for five dollars. It violates public school policy to charge students for required textbooks, so the next day I told students not to let the idea of having to purchase a copy influence their decision about whether they wanted to read *The Hunchback of Notre Dame*. I said I would buy extras and they had only to see me before class to obtain one.

Teaching is very messy indeed when students suddenly choose a novel you haven't read in a couple of decades and blithely expect you to take the book and run with it. What we discovered together was that compared with Mary Shelley's *Frankenstein*, Victor Hugo's *Hunchback* was a very easy read. With minimal scaffolding—I showed them the first ten minutes of the 1939 film version with Charles Laughton as

Quasimodo to give them a sense of the setting—students kept to a rigorous reading schedule of about thirty pages a night. The idea that they had chosen the book—that they had decided what was important—kept complaints to a minimum.

Our discussions of the book kept returning to a comparison of Quasimodo with Grendel and Frankenstein's monster (How is this like that?). Students drew parallels between Quasimodo's hopeless love for Esmeralda, Grendel's attraction to Wealthow in John Gardner's story, and Frankenstein's monster's desire for a female creature like himself. For sixteen-year-olds, such connections are like firecrackers going off in a chain. Once one student sees "how this is like that," others do too. I couldn't bear to ruin my students' enthusiasm for their ideas by assigning a formal analytical paper, so I came up with the following alternative writing assignment:

Culminating Assignment for Victor Hugo's
The Hunchback of Notre Dame:

In a beautifully written two-page paper, write the story of your reading of Victor Hugo's *The Hunchback of Notre Dame*. The following questions are meant to spur, not limit, your thinking. Feel free to ignore them and to respond in any way that fulfills the spirit of the assignment. Under no circumstances should you answer all these questions separately and in order. You should try to weave your responses into a seamless whole.

- What challenges did this text pose for you?
- What parts of the book did you find most moving, most intriguing, most unforgettable?
- How has your sojourn in Paris with Gringoire, Esmeralda, Quasimodo, and Claude Frollo changed you?
- Why would or wouldn't you choose to read another Victor Hugo novel?
- What questions do you still have about the story?
- Which character did you find the most compelling?
- Which ideas did you find the most compelling?
- How did you make time to read such a long novel? Was this difficult for you?

- What did reading *The Hunchback of Notre Dame* teach you about cathedrals, about human nature, about yourself? Did it teach you anything about reading?

The essays I received from this assignment were some of the best that students had written all semester. Instead of trying to second-guess what I wanted to see in a paper, they wrote about things that mattered to them. Janet Yu wrote, "I wasn't as keen as some of the other students to read *The Hunchback of Notre Dame* at first. I had seen the Disney movie and thought it was very bad. Victor Hugo's book was nothing like the film, though. I wonder if the scriptwriters read it at all. I suppose it's partly because I am hard of hearing that I related so much with Quasimodo. I kept thinking about how the bells were a great source of comfort to him in his silent world."

Other students wrote about how they were really proud of themselves for having read such a long book over a short period of time and how they felt more confident now about picking up heavy tomes. Nick Burleigh wrote that he thought he would probably want to write his term paper on Victor Hugo.

Outcomes That Can Never Be Predicted

So pleased was I with the tenth graders' papers on *The Hunchback of Notre Dame* that I decided to use a slightly modified list of questions for my twelfth-grade AP literature students' essays on *Crime and Punishment*. With five preparations a day, I often find myself mixing and matching assignments. Eric Bromberg, the author of the following essay, is an extraordinary student who I am quite sure will garner a four or five on the AP literature exam in May. He already earned a four last year on the AP language exam and wanted to try again this year to see if he could nail a five. Like many other high schools we offer an eleventh-grade honors American literature class that also prepares students for the AP language exam. The class' test differs from the exam in its focus on rhetoric and style.

Characterizing Eric in this manner raises another concern I have about teachers—myself included—instinctively equating student excellence with performance on AP tests. For all the good the College Board has done in terms of raising the level of instruction in senior English classes, I don't believe it should have a monopoly on how excellence is judged in high school English classrooms. Teachers need to reclaim this ground from test makers. Would Eric's essay earn a top score if judged according to an AP rubric? After reading his paper, I think you will see why I don't really care. Eric has demonstrated something in this essay that goes beyond any artificial measure or scoring guide.

I had asked Eric's AP class to read *Crime and Punishment* over our winter break and then to write a reflective essay using questions similar to the ones I had offered tenth graders for *The Hunchback of Notre Dame*. At first glance you might think that Eric's paper is simply a "snow job," casually written and demonstrating little hard evidence that he had read and analyzed the text. As his teacher, I had already gathered all the evidence I needed from classroom discussion in small and large groups to know that Eric had indeed read Dostoesvky with care. What I wanted to learn from this paper, and what Eric demonstrated so clearly, was how the book had affected him as a reader.

No Punishment Here

There is a difference between *Crime and Punishment* and every other book I've read, a distinction that gives this book exclusive shelf space as well as its own bookends. Often times when I read a good book, I can see the protagonist moving, talking, working, and thinking. I view the trees, the people, the weather, but always from about fourteen inches away from the page. My own surroundings, whether they consist of a bedroom, classroom, airplane, automobile, or wherever else I may be, are still intact. I'm still in California. I'm still hungry. I'm still reading a book. But, at a certain point during *Crime and Punishment*, I noticed that what Raskolnikov saw in front of him, I saw in front of me. When he turned a corner, I saw the buildings and people around that corner. At first, I thought fatigue was causing me to read in a half-dreaming state, a stupor that caused my local surroundings to mix and blur with nineteenth-century Russia. Then I realized I never fell asleep while reading. By the middle of Christmas vacation, when I was nearly two-thirds done with the book, I had to accept the bizarre phenomenon that a man can travel through St. Petersburg and look upon the city, breathe in its scent and feel it pulsating under his feet, while sitting comfortably in his bed at the same time. Of course this takes some getting used to.

The phenomenon I've described was a slow progression. The beginning of *Crime and Punishment* resembled many other books in terms of describing the scenery and introducing the characters. Soon, however, as Dostoevsky illustrated every string of emotion and web of thought in Raskolnikov's head, I began to pay special attention to each page of print, for I noticed I could relate to him as if he were my best friend. (This intense scrutinizing of text may have helped spur my experience.) On the second day of Christmas break I took a ski trip to Utah. During the bus ride, after being enraptured by my book for over an hour, Raskolnikov killed Alyona Ivanovna and her sister, Lizaveta. He had been planning it for some time now. After briefly panicking, Raskolnikov hesitated for a few seconds and as he began to leave the pawnbroker's shop, someone suddenly started walking up the stairs. He knew those footsteps were coming for him the minute they entered the building. Raskolnikov quickly locked the pawnbroker's door from the inside, (Stay calm!) crouched into a corner of the room, and waited in utter fear of being caught (not now, so soon after!). "The unknown man rang again, waited and suddenly tugged violently and impatiently at the handle of the door. Raskolnikov (I) gazed in horror at the hook shaking in its fastening, and . . . " blink, I realized there was a big-rig honking outside my window. In the distance, thick, lush trees stood upright. The mountains had become whiter, and seemed even further away than before. My right hand, which was holding a Coca-Cola, had squeezed the can into an hourglass shape. I looked around once again, at my friend next to me with headphones on, then at the blue seat cushion ahead of me with little red diamond patterns. I blinked again; and so it went. I had a 14-hour bus ride to Salt Lake City, ten hours of which were spent on Route 66 while the missing four hours were spent frantically walking around St. Petersburg, mostly avoiding human contact.

I wish I could define the magical gift of language Dostoevsky uses in *Crime and Punishment*. I also wish I had it. I believe it is an intangible, practically unattainable balance of words; somehow, he leaves nothing out that is needed. Never mind the brilliantly woven Biblical references and surnames that foreshadow character traits. Dostoevsky's exceptional talent is his ability to paint such a precise, realistic picture of the city and the people while exposing human emotions and behaviors with poetic accuracy. The reader has no choice but to animate the scene.

When asked by an *NEA Today* reporter where the standards movement falls short, Jonathan Kozol (2000) replied,

> The best things that happen in public schools are the outcomes that can never be predicted. The most beautiful discoveries students make are not like mountaintops that can be charted with maps, they're like crevices you won't really see until you are standing on top of them. The trouble with the standards movement is that you're so busy looking toward the next exam, you miss the crevices. The good news is that most good teachers find a way to deliver the skills without reducing classrooms to boot camps. (19)

I would like to think that my classroom, while a training ground for rigorous thinking and academic performance, has little in common with boot camp.

Three

Beyond Reading Standards

*A*ccording to English-Language Arts Content Standard 3.0 for California public schools, by grades nine and ten, "Students read and respond to historically or culturally significant works of literature that reflect and enhance their studies of history and social science. They conduct in-depth analyses of recurrent patterns and themes" (56).

Now compare that mandate with Annie Dillard's description of herself as a young reader (1987):

> Whenever I opened the book, the war struck up again, like a record whose music sounded when the needle hit. The skirling of Highlanders' bagpipes came playing again, high and thin over the dry oak ridges. The towheaded prisoner schoolchildren were just blabbing their memorized psalms when from right outside the greased parchment window sounded the wild and fatal whoops of Indian warriors on a raid.
>
> The wild and fatal whoops, the war whoops of the warriors, the red warriors whooping on a raid. It was a delirium. The tongue diddled the brain. Private life, book life, took place where words met imagination without passing through the world.
>
> I could dream it all whenever I wanted—and how often I wanted to dream it! Fiercely addicted, I dosed myself again and again with the drug of the dream.
>
> Parents have no idea what the children are up to in their bedrooms: They are reading the same paragraphs over and over in a stupor of violent bloodshed. Their legs are limp with horror. They hate the actual world. The actual world is a kind of tedious plane where dwells, and goes to school, the body, the boring body

which houses the eyes to read the books and houses the heart the books enflame. The very boring body seems to require an inordinately big, very boring world to keep it up, a world where you have to spend far too much time, have to *do* time like a prisoner, always looking for a chance to slip away, to escape back home to books, or escape back home to any concentration—fanciful, mental, or physical—where you can lose your self at last. (100)

Annie Dillard had clearly gone far beyond what California's reading standard describes, not only in terms of her obvious reading prowess but also in terms of the deep affinity she was developing for books. All the work to get children "reading by nine" (the motto of the *Los Angeles Times* reading initiative) will be for naught if young people aren't still reading at nineteen. Simply knowing how to read isn't enough. Kids need to acquire the reading habit.

Reading by Nine, Still Reading at Nineteen

Making reading happen in a culture where televisions are common fixtures in children's bedrooms and Buffy the Vampire Slayer a more familiar character than Sara, Plain and Tall isn't easy. Why should teenagers pick up Jon Krakauer's *Into Thin Air* and Sebastian Junger's *The Perfect Storm* when electronic games offer vicarious adventure galore? For anyone who would choose to read one of these adventure books, the answer is obvious. To most young people it is not.

Many children who know how to read seldom do. As a result, they never develop the fluency that would allow them to read with ease. The act never becomes effortless. Think about it. Working your way down this page doesn't feel like hard work. It feels like breathing. But children who are struggling to sound out words or make sense of the shape of a sentence find reading very hard work indeed. The skills you take for granted haven't yet become automatic for them.

Making the transition from knowing how to read to being able to read with ease takes practice. But if practicing resembles repeating piano scales to the beat of a metronome, only a dutiful few will ever become fluent readers. Practice needs to go hand-in-hand with pleasure—the special pleasure that only a good book can bring.

When I look for books to hook students who have yet to develop the reading habit, I try to find easy-to-read stories about hard-to-solve teenage problems. I also keep my eye out for the books that disappear from my classroom shelves. A few titles are impossible to hold onto. *The Guinness Book of World Records, Name Your Baby, Chicken Soup for the Teenage Soul,* and whatever Michael Crichton book has most recently been made into a movie all have a shelf life of under three days.

All copies of books by Francesca Lia Block quickly vanish without a trace. My favorite is *Missing Angel Juan,* the story of a tangly haired, purple-eyed teenager called Witch Baby who lives in L.A. and plays drums in a band called The Goat Guys. She also loves a boy named Angel Juan. When Angel leaves for New York, Witch Baby has to follow. Like Odysseus, she must venture into the unknown, face monsters beyond her ken, and descend into the underworld, all in order to save Angel Juan. Regardless of their understanding (or lack thereof) of epic motifs, teenagers resonate to this hero's tale. Maybe it is because the hero wears rollerskates.

In *Always Running, La Vida Loca: Gang Days in L.A.,* Luis Rodriguez describes his own coming of age in East L.A. This vivid memoir explores the lure of gang life and cautions against the violence that inevitably claims its participants. The text includes shockingly explicit passages (no doubt contributing to its popularity among teenage readers), but Rodriguez, himself a poet, uses his words to tell a shocking story.

What the disappearing books seem to have in common is that they portray young, contemporary protagonists caught up in a search for themselves. I like to think that it is not simply forgetfulness that causes my students to keep them, but rather a reluctance to part with a book that has, maybe for the first time, brought them the kind of pleasure that Annie Dillard describes.

Developing Reading Skills in Secondary Students

One of the most frustrating things about teaching high school is that many of us who teach English are and always have been addicted readers like Annie Dillard. We were attracted to the job by a fondness for young people and a love of books. Few high school English teachers expected that they would have to teach reading, as well.

One way to think about teaching reading skills to secondary students is to examine the behaviors of good readers when faced with difficult text. According to research by Pressley and Afflerbach (1995), excellent readers are actually quite strategic readers. As you look down this list, think about how many of these strategies you typically employ when you pick up a book.

According to Pressley and Afflerbach, excellent readers

1. overview before reading
2. look for important information in text and pay greater attention to it than other information
3. attempt to relate important points in text to one another to understand the text as a whole
4. activate and use prior knowledge to interpret text, such as generating hypotheses about text and predicting text content
5. reconsider and/or revise hypotheses about the meaning of text based on text content
6. reconsider and/or revise prior knowledge based on text content
7. relate text content to prior knowledge as part of constructing interpretations of text
8. attempt to infer information not explicitly stated in text when the information is critical to comprehension of the text
9. attempt to determine the meaning of words not understood or recognized, especially when a word seems critical to meaning construction

10. use strategies, such as underlining, repetition, making notes, visualizing, summarizing, paraphrasing, and self-questioning, to remember text

11. change reading strategies when comprehension is perceived not to be proceeding smoothly

12. evaluate the qualities of text, with these evaluations in part affecting whether text has impact on reader's knowledge, attitudes, behavior, etc.

13. reflect on and process text additionally after reading it (reviewing, questioning, summarizing, attempting to interpret, evaluating, considering alternative interpretations, considering how to process the text additionally, accepting one's understanding of the text, rejecting one's understanding of a text)

14. carry on a responsive conversation with the author

15. anticipate or plan for the use of knowledge gained from the reading.

Pressley and Afflerbach's final point about good readers planning for how they will use the new information they have garnered from a book reminds me of Deborah Meier's fifth habit-of-mind question: Why is this important? Who cares? Unless students see a use for what they read, whether imaginative or utilitarian, much of the print will pass by their eyes without much comprehension. I often have students who swear that they have done the homework reading, yet can't answer the simplest question about what happened on those pages. Their eyes did their duty, but their minds were not engaged.

Who Will Teach Them to Read?

Many high school English classes are full of students who do not have the basic reading skills to begin to employ the strategies Pressley and Afflerbach describe. These young people need help and they need it now. In current educational parlance, the buzzword for this help is *intervention*. Whatever schools choose to call it, and in my opinion whatever the cost, the help needs to be provided. If this means that some students enroll in two language arts classes at once—one for literature and composition, the other for reading—so be it. If a school decides that every ninth-grade English class should be a reading class, a remarkable model to examine is the Academic Literacy course developed by Ruth Schoenback, Cynthia Greenleaf, Christine Cziko, and Lori Hurwitz at Thurgood Marshall Academic High School in San Francisco.

As Cziko (1998) explains,

> The Academic Literacy course began as a ten-unit, year-long course for all Thurgood Marshall freshmen in the fall of 1996. Its purpose was to help the incoming students become higher level, strategic readers and to prepare them for the reading tasks they would encounter in high school and beyond. We knew that for students to become active readers, they had to first believe that reading with comprehension was something that could be learned; that it was not a mystery that you either "get" or "don't get," and that ninth grade was not too late to learn.
>
> We thought that if we could create classrooms in which students could use some of the energy they put into hiding what they don't understand into revealing and working to figure out their confusions we might create a powerful new learning dynamic. We thought about ways to make it "cool" to be able to articulate what in a particular text is confusing and why, and about how to invite the entire class to contribute strategies to unlock difficult text. It was crucial that all ninth-grade students took the course, so that strategies used by more successful students could be learned by all. The model would be teachers as "master readers" and students as "apprentice readers." This was not to be a remedial course. Finally, in order to make the course inquiry-based, we decided to create a curriculum in which the reading process itself was a subject of investigation. Using the common adolescent fascination with themselves, we hoped to help students develop metacognitive understandings by inviting them to look closely at their own reading and thinking processes. (7)

Students at Thurgood Marshall Academic High School have shown remarkable gains in their reading scores, but

Cziko and her colleagues continue to worry about building students' background knowledge, increasing their fluency, and developing their vocabulary, as well as developing their capacity to manage motivation for assigned rather than self-chosen readings. These teachers and researchers know they are on to something here, but they also understand that much remains to be done. Their book *Reading for Understanding: A Guide to Improving Reading in Middle and High School Classrooms* (Schoenback et al. 1999) offers an extraordinary window into a school where teenagers are learning to read.

The Academic Literacy course focuses on metacognition and uses an inquiry approach to explore key questions about reading: What is reading? What do proficient readers do when they read? Students are encouraged to explore their own reading process and thus gain a greater awareness of their reading and of the strategies that they use when they read. The course was also designed to increase students' motivation to read by helping them find personal enjoyment in reading and by convincing them of the power of literacy to shape their lives. The questions the course explores include What role does reading play in our personal and public lives? What role will reading play in my future educational and career goals? What goals can I set and work toward to help myself develop as a reader? Students revisit these questions throughout the course.

The course's key instructional strategies include sustained silent reading, reciprocal teaching, and explicit instruction in self-monitoring and cognitive techniques that facilitate reading a variety of texts. Students read a book of their choice for twenty to twenty-five minutes at least twice a week. They are required to read two hundred to three hundred pages each month, maintain a reflective reading log, and report and make a presentation on what was read. Reciprocal teaching is employed to improve students' comprehension. Groups of students read a common text and practice using the comprehension strategies of questioning, summarizing, predicting, and clarifying in the manner of competent readers. Specific instruction, as well as modeling and thinking aloud, is offered in note taking; paraphrasing; using graphic organizers and mapping; identifying root words, prefixes, and suffixes; and developing semantic networks.

A variety of assessments document the impact of the course. Students keep a log of the books they read. They assemble a reading portfolio, an individual reading plan, and a personal reading profile. The portfolio includes reflections, self-assessments, and an evaluation of their reading process. It also includes a record of the texts they read, and evidence of their use of a variety of reading comprehension strategies. Along with significantly raising reading scores on standardized text measures, the Academic Literacy course clearly demonstrates that ninth grade is not too late to intervene.

The aspect of this work that I find most powerful is that Cziko and her colleagues haven't oversimplified the act of reading by reducing it to a list of skills to be acquired or of increasingly difficult texts to be mastered.

Consider the Oyster

Sugar, hydrogenated vegetable shortening, thiamine, enriched wheat flour, cocoa, glycerine. However detailed the list of ingredients, they simply do not add up to a Girl Scout Thin Mint. Step-by-step instructions for putting the ingredients together don't re-create the morsel for me, either. To make that cookie come alive I need a less analytical, more imaginative description. I need something like what M. F. K. Fisher wrote about oysters (1988): "Southern oysters are more like the Southern ladies than the brisk New Englanders. They are delicate and listless. Further north men choose their oysters without sauce. They like them cold, straightforward, simple, capable of spirit but unadorned" (42). Fanciful? Maybe. But when pursuing a complex subject, a flight of fancy is sometimes necessary.

Like the taste of an oyster, literacy is difficult to describe without resort to metaphor. No sequence of lessons, however detailed, can begin to describe the complex behavior involved when a reader meets a book. For example, there is the reader's relationship to the subject to consider. Is this a familiar or unfamiliar story? Are the events described in the book something the reader can recognize? Does the reader have a feeling for what kind of text this is—a romance novel, a position paper, a fairy tale, a letter? What attitude toward books has the reader seen modeled by parents and friends? Does the reader want to know what is written in the book? I believe the answers to these questions affect our students' ability to read a text every bit as much as their mechanical and more measurable reading skills do.

Emily Dickinson called reading a frugal chariot that "bears the Human soul." Her metaphor comes closer to describing literacy than any catalog of book titles or list of basic skills ever could. Comparing literature with various means of transportation works for me because I am convinced that children who don't earn their "license to read" face a dismal road. Acquiring reading skills can be difficult, however, unless a young reader simultaneously develops a reader's habits of mind. Children need to learn about the adventure of reading as much as they need to learn the alphabet. Without the desire to figure out what is coded on the page, the child may not bother. Without a book he wants to read, the child may never try.

The Bad Habits of Good Readers

One area that I think deserves the attention of reading researchers is a study of so-called good readers' bad habits. While applauding the Thurgood Marshall Academic High School's model of teachers as master readers and students as apprentices, it seems to me that we would do well to examine what compulsive readers actually do. Most people envy compulsive readers. In the time it takes an average reader to finish one book, they have read several. Watching such readers devour an armload of books a week, it is hard not to grow resentful. But before placing compulsive readers on a pedestal and training all students to race through text, we need to consider the bad habits of many good readers. What do compulsive readers do that is so different? How do they get through all those books?

Speaking from my own experience as a compulsive reader as well as my observations of many students I have known, I can say with reasonable assurance that avid readers don't always make the most of the books that pass through their hands. Here's why: Compulsive readers often

- Value speed over reflection. Such readers seldom pause between books to think about what they have read. They reach for the next one without taking a breath.
- Skip anything they think might be boring. Unlike "inexpert" readers, these speed readers feel free to sidestep any passage that interrupts the flow of a story. They skim descriptive pages and skip altogether imbedded poetry or quotations, such as the medieval tale within Edgar Allan Poe's "Fall of the House of Usher." When I read A. S. Byatt's literary thriller *Possession*, I ignored all the Browning-like and Rossetti-like poetry that Byatt so artfully wove through the novel. It wasn't until a scholarly friend remarked that the contemporary Victorian poems were the most extraordinary aspect of the book that I sheepishly returned to read them through.
- Care more about their personal reading than assigned reading. I have known many students who perform very poorly in high school, preferring to prop the latest Barbara Kingsolver novel inside their textbook and simply read their way through the school day.
- Declare a text they don't care for to be "boring" with great authority. This can be enormously disruptive in the classroom. When students who have read a scant five pages of *A Tale of Two Cities* hear a classmate who finished the book over the weekend say that it "sucks," they stop reading.
- Rush through writing assignments in order to get back to their book. As a result, these readers are often poor writers and careless spellers. Wide reading gives avid readers knowledge of many things, and allows them to dash off

something that passes muster, but these students are reluctant to spend the kind of time revising that would make the quality of their writing equal to the quality of their thinking.

- Can get stuck reading one particular genre for a very long time. For some this might mean a summer of Albert Payson Terhune dog books. For others it might mean a six-month diet of Ayn Rand. As Lynne Sharon Schwartz writes in *Ruined by Reading* (1996), "I read every novel by Jean Rhys and Barbara Pym as soon as I could get my hands on them. It was like eating candy—the chocolate-covered nuts of the cinema or the celebrated potato chips of which you can't eat just one. The variations in their novels were, in fact, no more than the slightly different planes and convolutions in each potato chip, and each one predictably tasty. I became an expert in self-indulgence" (103).

While avid readers often achieve the highest levels on standardized tests, I believe that with guidance they can become more thoughtful readers. I recall my own first reading of Zora Neal Hurston's *Their Eyes Were Watching God*. As usual, I had barreled through the novel at breakneck speed and went to my book club meeting wondering what all the fuss was about. Fortunately I didn't make a fool of myself (as I might have done at sixteen) by declaring the book boring. Instead I kept my mouth shut and listened to what other readers had to say. It dawned on me as they spoke with such insight of Janie Crawford's travels being a classic hero's journey that as I raced through the book, I had missed a quite a lot. It seemed, in fact, that I had missed it all. The best thing about being an avid reader, of course, is that rereading a book isn't a problem. I don't exactly know how, but constant readers always seem to find time where others find none.

Reading Above the Rim

For every grade level from K through 12, California's 1997 *English Language Arts Content Standards* refer to a document called *Recommended Readings in Literature* as a source for books that "illustrate the quality and complexity of the materials to be read by students." The only problem with this statement is that at the time the standards were published, that document didn't exist. Two years (and many committee meetings) later, "the list" is taking shape.

I was lucky to be one of the thirty teachers and librarians assigned the happy task of recommending titles for California's list. At first I was tempted to submit only titles that no one else had heard of. Wasn't the invitation proof of my reading prowess? Why not show off? Fortunately my fit of reader's snobbery passed, and I began to think long and hard about exactly which kind of books belonged on a list that would have such stature and influence.

The books most certainly had to have literary merit. They must be sturdy stories that could withstand both haphazard and laborious readings, books that wouldn't wilt in readers' hands. The books should challenge readers to consider a world unlike the one they know. Ideally, they would lure readers into unfamiliar times and places with luscious prose. Young readers would suffer and triumph with characters unlike any they meet in real life. I know that I have a more intimate relationship with certain characters I met between the pages of a book than with many people I have known for years. I decided that the books I would recommend for this list had to be luminous things, capable of transforming ordinary mortals into angels.

While others argued for books that students liked, I found myself suggesting books that would give teenagers trouble, ornery books that would disturb them as they read. I tried to think of books that had had that effect on me. *Crime and Punishment, The Magic Mountain, War and Peace, Blood Meridian, The Sound and the Fury,* and *Beloved* immediately sprang to mind. I am quite sure I am a different person for having read these books. Whether for better or worse is hard to say, but that I am changed forever is certain.

I then tried to think of books a bit less intimidating but that would still cause students to stretch. Here is the list I submitted:

39

Twenty Novels Guaranteed to Give a Teenager Pause

Bastard Out of Carolina by Dorothy Allison

The Handmaid's Tale by Margaret Atwood

Hunger by Lan Samantha Chan

Waiting for the Barbarians by J. M. Coetze

White Noise by Don Delillo

Blue Raft Over Yellow Water by Michael Dorris

Birdsong by Sebastian Faulks

A Lesson Before Dying by Ernest Gaines

My Son's Story by Nadine Gordimer

Narcissus and Goldmund by Herman Hesse

A Prayer for Owen Meany by John Irving

One Flew Over the Cuckoo's Nest by Ken Kesey

Always Outnumbered, Always Outgunned by Walter Mosley

Bone by Fae Myenne Ng

The Things They Carried by Tim O'Brien

Sula by Toni Morrison

Imagining Argentina by Lawrence Thornton

Johnny Got His Gun by Dalton Trumbo

Sacred Hunger by Barry Unsworth

Philadelphia Fire by John Edgar Wideman

While there might not seem much coherence to such a list of titles, I believe that when offered a steady diet of extraordinary books, teenagers can't but help but mature. It's not that I don't want young people to enjoy the oblivion of their adolescence. I just want them to see more.

I have never actually taught a single one of these books to a whole class. Many contain scenes that could be problematic in terms of sex, violence, or strong language. While the community I teach in is relatively liberal, district rules mandate that if a teacher plans to purchase more than five copies, a book must be formally adopted by the board of education. What I do is put these novels into the hands of single readers I know can handle powerful stories, or use them with small groups of students in literature circles. Invariably the single readers come back desperate to talk with someone about what they've just read and not quite yet digested.

I consider knowing which books to hand students who read above the rim as important a part of my teaching responsibility as knowing how to scaffold instruction for those who struggle. Committed young readers need books and book recommendations the way committed young athletes need equipment and courts. Of course it's seldom possible for classroom teachers to keep up with new books the way we would like, but the Internet has put help at our fingertips. An extraordinary example of what I am referring to is Berkeley Public Library Teen Services. Its website offers annotated book recommendations under engaging headings like "First Person Youthful," "Boys to Men," "Stranger in a New Land," and "On the Road." Go to http://www.infopeople.org/bpl/teen/booklist.html and see for yourself. Another rich source for book recommendations is the American Library Association Notable Books list at http://www.ala.org/rusa/notable99.html.

Four

Beyond Writing Standards

Students will write compositions with a clear focus, logically related ideas to develop it, and adequate detail.

(Massachusetts Learning Standard 19, Composition Strand)

Dear Mrs. Jago,

I learned alot in this class. this class made me use parts of my mind that I didnt really use before. I also liked most of the assignments we had. I just hope I pass this class to graduate. I love being in your class. I wouldn't change it for nothing.

Sincerely,
Jorge C.

Jorge is seventeen years old and the product of thirteen years of public education. The note appears exactly as he wrote it. If this isn't evidence of malpractice, including my own, I don't know what more evidence one needs. "Alot"? No capital letter at the beginning of a sentence? Contractions without an apostrophe? A generation of students who have not acquired the rudiments of correct usage is passing through our schools. No wonder so many students need remedial English as freshmen in college. No wonder their employers are hopping mad.

Jorge and the Jungle of Public Education

I can offer plenty of excuses; for example, there were thirty-nine students enrolled in Jorge's senior English class, making it difficult for me to get around to each one individually. I can also point to his spotty attendance or casual attitude toward academics. If I really want to delude myself, I can blame Jorge's lack of skills on the fact that he speaks Spanish at home or that his family is relatively poor. The no-fault truth is that Jorge has been shortchanged. He came to the public schools for an education, and we let him graduate with writing skills no reasonable person would tolerate from a sixth grader.

In a speech to the National Coalition of Education Activists, author Luis Rodriguez compared his own education in Los Angeles public schools with the education's received by more privileged students in Bryn Mawr, Pennsylvania, where he had been hired as a poet in residence. "Why was it that these schools had a 100 percent graduation rate and a 100 percent college entrance rate? What is it about these kids that they cannot fail? I asked the teachers and they told me that these children feel more than empowered; they feel that they are entitled. Their school won't let them fail. The kids are not any more intelligent or creative than other kids. But somebody ensures that none will fail. There is a sense that the entire institution will, if necessary, come together for the needs of just one kid."

This is the way it should be for all children. But the money California spends per student simply will not buy what a seventeen-thousand-dollar-a-year private tuition offers students in Bryn Mawr. Money alone will not solve the problems of public education, particularly if it's squandered on bureaucratic nest building, but money can help. It can buy smaller class sizes and a tutor for Jorge. It can put computers in every classroom and clean rest rooms in every school. It can buy books. Money can also buy better-trained teachers and reward effective instructors for a job well done.

When the results of the Stanford 9—a standardized test that every second through eleventh grader in California must sit for—are published in the newspaper, people start pointing fingers. It's the fault of bilingual education. It's the fault of not enough bilingual education. It's uncredentialed young teachers. It's burned-out old teachers. I don't care whose fault it is.

I just want a system that will come together when necessary for the sake of a single child. I want an institution, like the one in Bryn Mawr, that will not allow its students to fail.

Jorge's parents put their faith in the public school system and counted on our professional expertise to ensure that he would be prepared for life after high school. They expected, and had a right to expect, that his teachers would make sure Jorge learned to write. I, along with others, have signally failed their child.

NAEP Writing Standards

With great regularity, newspaper headlines proclaim our children's failure: "1 in 4 U.S. Students Has Proficiency in Writing." This particular headline referred to the National Assessment of Educational Progress (NAEP) scores in writing for students in the fourth, eighth, and twelfth grades. What dismayed me about the coverage was that the story included no explanation of what it takes for a student to be designated "proficient" on this rigorous test.

According to the NAEP, eighth-grade students performing at the proficient level should be able to

- Create an effective response to the task in form, content, and language.
- Express analytical, critical, and/or creative thinking.
- Demonstrate an awareness of the purpose and intended audience.
- Have logical and observable organization appropriate to the task.
- Show effective use of transitional elements.
- Use sufficient elaboration to clarify and enhance the central idea.
- Use language (e.g., variety of word choice and sentence structure) appropriate to the task.
- Have few errors in spelling, grammar, punctuation, and capitalization that interfere with communication.

I applaud the high standards that the NAEP sets for student writing. I also think it is essential for parents and policymakers to understand exactly how high the national bar has been set. Do you think your own writing would be considered proficient under these guidelines?

No English teacher I know would claim that more than one out of four students in a typical class is currently able to write at what the NAEP describes as the proficient level. We are working to help students reach these standards, but we ourselves need help. Classes of thirty-six students are common in California middle and high schools. The three states that scored above the national average on this writing assessment in 1998—Connecticut, Maine, and Massachusetts—have fewer than twenty-five students in a class. They also spend over one thousand dollars per child per year more on education than we in the Golden State do. Money alone won't solve the problem, but it can help.

High school English teachers also need help from their colleagues. If students write only in English classes, they will never produce enough prose to develop as writers. I believe students from sixth grade on should be responsible for writing a two- to three-page essay every week. One week the paper could be for English class, the next week for history. And students need timely feedback on what they produce. Peer response can sometimes be helpful on rough drafts, but students need a teacher's comments and constructive criticism in order to become proficient.

No writing teacher who is responsible for 150 students a day can possibly do her job well. I have friends, good teachers, who left the profession over the paper load. The National Council of Teachers of English has long recommended that English teachers should meet no more than eighty students a day. Even that number is a challenge, but it would allow teachers to assign the amount of writing students need to be doing and still get papers back to kids in a reasonable amount of time.

Is it possible for all California students to become proficient writers? We'll never know until every child has a teacher with the time and expertise to do the job right.

Responding to Student Writing

Stories like Jorge's are part of what has driven the standards movement. Believing that coherent instruction can be mandated, states have rushed to create a series of increasingly more difficult benchmarks that students must reach or be held back. In terms of sentence structure, California's seventh-grade students must "Place modifiers properly and use the active voice." By eighth grade they must "Use correct and varied sentence types and sentence openings to present a lively and effective personal style." By ninth grade they must "Identify and correctly use clauses, phrases, and mechanics of punctuation." The logic of such a plan seems irrefutable. The problem is that learning to write is a messy business. No list of skills can ever capture all that a teacher needs to know about teaching writing.

Remember how you learned to ride a bike? Mom or Dad . held the handlebars with one hand and the wobbly seat with the other. Urging you to pedal, this trusty helper showered you with encouragement. "Good girl. A little faster now. You can do it. Keep going. Good. You've got it!" You can probably still remember the happy day when you sailed off alone on that two-wheeler. Hours, years of cycling pleasure followed. On a fine Sunday, the bike path may still beckon.

Now think about how you were taught to write. Your teacher assigned a paper. You struggled for a few hours, filling the pages as best you could, and turned in the paper the following morning. The essay came back bleeding red ink with teacher's comments like "Weak thesis," "Inadequate evidence," "Shallow interpretation," "Superficial treatment of this subject." The ubiquitous "awk" was sprinkled throughout the paper. With this validation of the incompetence you had been feeling, you decided that you agreed with the teacher. You are a lousy writer. Her annotations proved it.

Although a critical approach to teaching writing is meant to encourage excellence, it can sometimes discourage students forever. It can also turn what should be an intellectually stimulating activity for both student and teacher into a hated task. This does not mean kids should be praised for turning in drivel or that the teacher should refrain from circling errors for fear of hurting students' feelings. Nothing is more damaging to an emerging writer than a vague "Well done!" and an A on a paper that is full of spelling mistakes or incomplete. Such grading is also dishonest.

When reading student papers, I try to balance my criticism with encouragement. I believe young writers learn as much from my pointing out a sentence that sings or a sharply supported point as they do from my teacherly complaints about split infinitives and faulty parallelism. I also think that students can take in only so many criticisms at once. As with learning to ride a bicycle, there are so many things to do at once in writing that at first it seems impossible that you will ever get it right. Remember how you used to overcorrect when steering? Or how when you got scared you slowed down so much you toppled? It's the same for young writers.

"Good opening line, Yolanda." "Keep writing about this point. I want to know more." "This needs another draft, Jeremy. You don't want me to put a grade on this." "Could you insert another quote here? If you can't find one, how about another example?" "I love this sentence, Amos, but it belongs at the beginning, not the end, of your paper."

In so many words, what I try to say to students is "Keep pedaling." Keep pedaling, and your sense of how it feels to get it right on paper will develop. Keep pedaling, and you will inevitably find yourself picking up speed. Keep pedaling, and, though you may come across rough spots on the road and even take a few spills, the ride is worth it. Keep pedaling, not for me but for you.

Some Elements Never Go Out of Style

The Elements of Style, by William Strunk Jr. and E. B. White, was recently named by New York City librarians as one of the Twenty-one Classics for the Twenty-first Century. Who would have thought this slim volume of advice about writing, now in its fourth edition, would garner such acclaim, particularly at a time when "anything goes" seems to be so many writers' style of choice? Maybe it has something to do with—dare I say it—good writing.

Since it was first published by Macmillan in 1959, *The Elements of Style* has sold ten million copies. The book was the brainchild of William Strunk, who wrote it as a guidebook for his students at Cornell. The professor died in 1946, and one of the students who benefited from his tuition, E. B. White (beloved author of *Charlotte's Web*) took the manuscript and gave us not only a handbook for good writing, but one of the best examples of good writing around.

Take this tidbit of simple advice: "Write with nouns and verbs." I cannot count the number of times I have written on student papers "Avoid adverbs. Find a stronger verb." Novice writers sprinkle their essays with "really" and "very" hoping to bolster weak verbs. Though some may feel that Strunk and White's injunctions limit their range, I have always found them liberating. "Never tack -*ize* onto a noun to create a verb. Usually you will discover that a useful verb already exists. Why use 'moisturize' when there is the simple, unpretentious word *moisten*?"

The underlying purpose of reminders like "Use orthodox spelling" and "Do not overwrite" is consideration for the reader. While others might seek to dazzle with flights of creative fancy, Strunk and White championed what some call the American plain style, which consists of sentences that are uninterrupted by secondary clauses and whose subject, verb, and object are bound closely together. I can think of no better style for students to emulate.

White's ruminative closing section has been left intact in the fourth edition. In it, this paragon of prose advises writers that "There is simply a better chance of doing well if the writer holds a steady course, enters the stream of English quietly, and does not thrash about." I plan to use that phrase on the student papers that are sitting next to me here, waiting to be corrected. "Less thrashing about, please, Eric." It's good advice for teenagers' writing and, whether or not White intended this, even better advice for their lives.

Teaching Teenagers to Revise

In her book of "instructions on writing and life," *Bird by Bird*, Anne Lamott dispels the illusion that perfect prose drips naturally from anyone's pen. "People tend to look at successful writers, writers who are getting their books published and maybe even doing well financially, and think that they sit down at their desks every morning feeling like a million dollars, feeling great about who they are and how much talent they have and what a great story they have to tell; that they take in a few deep breaths, push back their sleeves, roll their necks a few times to get all the cricks out, and dive in, typing fully formed passages as fast as a court reporter" (1994, 21).

Anyone who writes would find such a picture laughable, but student writers assume that this is exactly how writing works. When they can't produce a first draft that earns more than a C from their teacher, they take this to mean that they are no good at writing. Revision? What's that? They understand about recopying to tidy up the handwriting or maybe running a spell-check program on their computers, but the kind of revision that involves a rethinking of content and a reshaping of sentences is inconceivable to them.

For years writing teachers have tried to formulate lessons in which students edit one another's papers, offering suggestions for improvement and helping one another spot errors, but this can result in the blind leading the blind. It also tends to annoy the better writers in the class, who pore over a classmate's paper with great care only to have their own draft given a cursory glance and token "good" scribbled at the bottom. I continue to use peer editing with students, but I now ask them to focus on content rather than mechanics, and I try to pair students so as not to penalize the diligent.

Looking for other ways to move apprentice writers from a sorry first draft to a more accomplished final copy, I began experimenting with self-editing strategies. After all, most writers don't have the luxury of a colleague to read their work in progress. Revision is lonely work.

Before I begin to describe this revision strategy, I want to emphasize that I wouldn't use it more than once during a school year. Part of the activity's effectiveness is its novelty. When students arrive on Monday morning with first drafts of their essays, I hand out crayons. (This in itself gets students' attention, something that is not easy to do with teenagers at 8:15 A.M.) I then proceed to take them step-by-step through the following instructions:

- Circle in orange all "to be" verbs (*is, are, was, were, am*).
- Underline in blue any sentences that begin with "There is/are."
- Cross out in brown every "I think" or "in my opinion."
- Find the longest sentence in your draft. Underline it in red.
- Find the shortest sentence in your draft. Underline it in green.
- Choose your favorite phrase, sentence, or passage in what you wrote. Color it yellow.
- Find the clumsiest part of your draft and underline it in black.

After we have had fun with all the colors, I ask students to think about what aspects of revision each of the colors represents. In this manner they begin to internalize the various purposes of revision and come to see that the process involves much more than simply fixing mistakes. Students begin to see that a paper full of "to be" verbs hasn't taken full advantage of the glorious range of verbs available in English. We talk about how important variety in sentence openings is for reader interest. Who would want to read an essay where every other sentence begins with "There is"?

No matter how many times I have explained that an essay is their own opinion, the "I think's" still creep in. Crossing them out helps students notice how well their sentences can stand without these unnecessary phrases. Identifying the long and short sentences allows students to see whether they have employed any variety in sentence length. I urge them to insert one three-word sentence for punch.

I then ask for volunteers to put sentences that need help on the board. Together we make suggestions for revisions, always leaving final decisions about what will ultimately appear in a paper up to the writer. When the bell rings to signal the end of the period, everyone in the room has a good idea of how his or her draft can be improved.

As Anne Lamott (1994, 25) explains, "Almost all good writing begins with terrible first efforts. You need to start somewhere. Start by getting something—anything—down on paper. A friend of mine says that the first draft is the down draft—you just get it down. The second draft is the up draft—you fix it up. You try to say what you have to say more accurately. And the third draft is the dental draft, where you check every tooth, to see if it's loose or cramped or decayed, or even, God help us, healthy."

By helping students self-edit, I'm hoping to provide them with the skills they need to give their drafts a checkup.

Why Students Need Creative Writing

Even though I teach a senior creative writing course, I have always been skeptical of creative writing assignments in English classes. Who has time for them with two epics, three plays, and fifteen novels to read and ten analytical essays to write in any school year? There is no room to play. While such a heavy load may seem inconceivable for non–honors students, I believe we must find ways for all students to read and write much more than they currently do. Our English department guidelines state that all ninth through twelfth graders, whatever their level, should be reading one book outside class every three weeks and one book inside class every six weeks, and should write at least one analytical essay each grading period. Such guidelines are impossible to enforce, of course, but at least we know the standard of work to which we are trying to hold both ourselves and our students.

California Language Arts Standard 2.1 mandates that students should "Write biographical or autobiographical narratives or short stories," but I rarely offer my tenth-grade students opportunities for creative assignments, especially anything that would require extended attention. I must also confess that I feel at sea assigning grades to teenagers' stories. What criteria apply?

Two things happened recently that have me reconsidering this stance. In his writer's notebook, Jed Oppenheim, a senior in the creative writing class, explained that during the last few years he had felt that he had begun to lose touch with his creative side. He said how much he was enjoying being in a creative writing class and how good it felt to begin exercising his imagination once more. He felt that his imagination had grown rusty. Given the curriculum that most sophomores and juniors work through in order to prepare themselves for college, Jed's observation did not surprise me. It made me feel guilty.

I thought of the short pieces Jed's classmates had written the day before, when I asked them to describe an emotion in terms of one of their senses. My counterintuitive instructions caused students to stretch as writers and to say something fresh about what could be an otherwise stale subject. Brian Vasquez wrote, "The sound of fear is like footsteps on a creaky wooden floor. The whole world has shut up for just those footsteps. Your heart seems to leap out in front of you until you find it and the footsteps have begun beating in time."

Jonathan Guzman wrote, "Loneliness tastes like a stick of gum. You think you can cope with it because like gum it tastes sweet and flavorful at first. But as time progresses there is less and less sweetness. As loneliness matures in your mouth you strive to chew what little sweetness remains in the wad. You realize it tastes of nothing. But not until you've chewed loneliness for a long, long while." Brian's and Jonathan's powerful descriptions clearly met the dictates of California Language Arts Standard 2.1e, "Make effective use of descriptions of appearance, images, shifting perspectives, and sensory details."

With Jed's comment about the need to educate students' imaginations still ringing in my ears, I saw that my son had come home with a creative writing assignment from his ninth-grade English teacher. I wrinkled my nose. James needs practice with essays, I thought. He should be reading more. What's the point of his writing a juvenile adventure story? But James' enthusiasm for the project was unbounded. He told versions of his story over and over whenever he could find someone to listen. He kept changing characters' names until they sounded just right to him. He wrote dialogue for odd, medieval creatures and then checked to see how the words sounded out loud.

To my mind the tale was obviously derivative of the fantasy books he had been reading, but to James it was utterly new, a story never told quite this way before. As he put words to paper I noticed that he cared a great deal about getting them down just right. He would bound out of his room asking, "Now what's the word for . . . ?" Going from a handwritten to a typed copy, he revised much more than I had seen him do for other assignments. He also took chances with diction and tone that were surprisingly sophisticated. I began to speculate that the occasional creative assignment might be of value to a novice writer, especially in terms of fostering a positive attitude toward writing.

I also noticed that just as my creative writing students' products demonstrated mastery of writing standard 2.1e, so had James' story met the demands of 2.1 a–d:

- Relate a sequence of events and communicate the significance of the events to the audience.

- Locate scenes and incidents in specific places.
- Describe with concrete sensory details the sights, sounds, and smells of a scene and the specific actions, movements, gestures, and feelings of the characters; use interior monologue to depict the character's feelings.
- Pace the presentation of actions to accommodate changes in time and mood.

Watching my twelfth-grade creative writing students compose with delight, I thought about how, in the pursuit of intellectual rigor, I had denied students this pleasure for the last few years. Why should students have to wait for the homestretch of their high school education to be allowed to invent and imagine? How much would it hurt to read one fewer book and instead write a story of their own?

Five

Beyond Research Standards

*E*very standards document contains references to student research. As a result, the term paper has once again reared its head in the high school English curriculum. I would like to suggest ways to redesign this assignment so that it takes advantage of the wealth of information available to student researchers on the Internet, and at the same time encourages excellence by allowing students multiple options for presenting their findings.

One of the curious things about writing often for publication is that you leave a paper trail and inevitably, over time, contradict yourself. In the years that I have written about education, I have had occasion to say many dramatic things, some of which I later regretted, others of which I wish I could revise. What I would like to tinker with now is my previous stand on the abolition of the term paper.

Reconsidering Student Research

The title of my 1990 essay "Death Comes to the Term Paper, or the Extinction of Termapapersaurus Rex" still appeals to me aesthetically, but I now disagree with my premise. We need to resuscitate the beast. What I objected to ten years ago was the way term paper projects ate up instructional time. Today computers have eliminated much of the busywork that used to go into generating a typed paper, and Internet access has made genuine student research possible. The term paper is dead. Long live the term paper.

Technology has made research sexy. Students who would never in their lives delve into tomes of the *Reader's Guide to Periodical Literature* now find manipulating a search engine a cool thing to do, not a bit nerdy. No longer is the preparation of a footnoted manuscript a laborious task, because most students are reasonably able on a keyboard and style guidelines for citing sources have been sensibly simplified.

The benefits of a term paper assignment remain the same. Students learn how to search for information and come to know their chosen subject in depth. Students also have a finished product they can point to with pride. Unfortunately, there are some new hazards. Electronic research can be enormously time-consuming, and students can easily become overwhelmed with useless data. In order to help novices avoid getting tangled in the Web, I remind them

- To examine websites for clues to their reliability. University, government, and museum websites are often excellent sources of sound information.
- To use several search engines. I find Google and AltaVista particularly useful for student research.
- To be sure to explore subscription databases (such as GALEnet, InfoTrac, and Proquest) on school or public library computers.
- To work with a partner and ask for help at the reference desk of the library when they get stuck or lost.
- Not to rely solely upon electronic sources. Books often provide more in-depth information on a topic than any website does. The Internet can, however, be a way to find the books you need.
- Not to be distracted by bells and whistles. The most valuable sites are often relatively unadorned.

The English-Language Arts Content Standards for California Public Schools recommend that students learn to "understand the structure and organization of various reference materials" beginning in the third grade. By ninth grade, students are expected to be able to "use clear research questions and suitable research methods to elicit and present evidence from primary and secondary sources" and to "synthesize information from multiple sources and identify complexities and discrepancies in the information and the different perspectives found in each medium."

If we want our children to meet these rigorous standards, they are going to have to write term papers. What makes the best sense is to have the assignment move across the disciplines—one year in science, the next in history, the following year in English. But however schools organize the task, the message from standards documents is clear: Research is an essential skill that all children must acquire.

Steps in the Research Process

For a class of ninth graders with below-average writing skills and minimal enthusiasm for reading, I developed the following research paper guidelines. We had to work together for several days brainstorming the names of individuals whose achievements would be worthy of research, but the time spent was a good investment in the assignment.

Research Paper Guidelines
Ninth-Grade English

Purpose

The purpose of this project is to develop your research skills while learning about how a historical character has metaphorically "climbed the highest mountain." Your term paper will be a record of your research as well as a personal reflection about what it means to struggle and attain a difficult goal.

Steps in the Process

- Read the first pages of Jon Krakauer's memoir *Into Thin Air.* Discuss why individuals choose to "climb the highest mountain" even when it puts them in such personal danger.

Brainstorm other historical figures that have metaphorically done the same.

- Choose an individual to research. Go to the library and find information about this person. You must read at least one full biography or memoir.
- Check on the Internet for information about this person. Many famous individuals have their own Web pages. Keep detailed notes of what you find.
- Read what you have found and while you read look for connections to our controlling theme. How has this individual climbed the highest mountain?
- Write a four- to five-page draft exploring how the person you have researched has been attracted to or forced to deal with a particular problem or challenge and how he or she has met this challenge. Be sure that you discuss the theme of climbing the highest mountain in your introduction. In your conclusion, return to this theme and offer food for thought to your reader. How has learning about this person affected your own ideas about climbing the highest mountain?
- Have critical friends read your draft. Revise. Edit.
- Present your final copy, which includes the essay, a title page, citations within the text, and a works cited page. Models for each of these pages will be provided. Please observe the following due dates:
  Individual chosen: _____
  Research completed: _____
  Draft completed: _____
  Final copy turned in: _____

I find it helps to send a letter about the assignment home to parents.

Dear Parents,

Over the next two months, your child will be embarking upon a research paper project. I have received a great deal of feedback from former students about how important this experience is to prepare them for writing long papers in college. I think the research aspect of the assignment will also be a tremendously exciting intellectual challenge.

It would help me a great deal if you could review the attached guidelines and talk with your child periodically about his or her progress. Please don't hesitate to call me at school or to find me online at jago@gseis.ucla.edu if you have any questions.

Sincerely,
Carol Jago

For a tenth-grade honors class, I altered the guidelines in order to have students focus on one author. Given these students' greater facility with both writing and reading, I wanted to push them to begin to think like literary scholars.

Research Paper Guidelines
Tenth-Grade Honors English

Purpose

The purpose of this project is to explore in depth the work of a writer whose prose and themes intrigue you. Choose an author whose work you have already enjoyed, read two other books by this author, and research related biographical and critical sources. Your term paper will be a record of your research as well as a personal reflection upon this writer's work.

Steps in the Process

- Choose an author whose work you admire from your previous reading. You may choose someone from our fall outside reading list, someone whose work we have studied in class, or someone from your own independent reading.
- Find and read two other books by this author. Ask for suggestions for titles.
- Go to the library and research biographical information on your author both in reference books and on the Internet. Keep detailed notes or print pages of what you find.

- Go to the library and find critical essays about your author's work, specifically about the novels you have read. Read these and take notes on how the critic's interpretation expanded or contradicted your own reading of the work.
- Construct a working thesis for your paper. Your thesis should be the answer to a provocative question about this writer's work.
- Create an organizational plan for your paper. Some things to consider: Should the biographical information appear first or would it be more effective woven throughout the paper? How big a part will quotes play in your paper? Will you discuss the novels separately or will you focus on themes or issues and then discuss these in terms of the author's body of work?
- Draft your essay. The paper should be five to seven pages long (longer if you use extended quotes). Be sure to explore the reasons you chose this author. What fascinates you about his or her writing? What made you want to read more? Is there any connection between the author's life and his or her work? How have the critical essays you've read opened up new ways of thinking about these novels for you? What questions do you have that your research has not been able to answer?
- Have your draft read by several critical friends. Revise. Revise. Revise.
- Present your final copy, which includes the essay, a title page, citations within the text, and a works cited page. Models for each of these pages will be provided.

A common complaint from students who chose a contemporary author is that they can find no critical essays. Instead of sending these students back to the library, we sit down together at a computer. I can often help them find magazine reviews or other "semicritical" commentary on the author's work. Although what we find may not fall under the category of scholarly analysis, it can still give students an insight into what others have written about their author.

Students Assess the Assignment

At the completion of a literary research project, I asked my tenth graders to be candid with me about what they thought of the assignment. While fifteen-year-olds are far from experts on the subject of either research or standards, my students have strong feelings about any misuse of their time. The week in February that they refer to in their responses was a series of pupil-free days my district had set aside for professional development. I made the paper's due date the day students returned from this break.

Dan Nabel wrote one of the more scholarly papers, on symbolism in two William Faulkner short stories.

> I think that doing a research paper is a good idea; it gives us experience with such a thing—I mean, we've never written anything this long before and it's good to have exposure to it. I really liked being able to choose pretty much everything about the paper—who we got to do it on, and what WE wanted to write about. I think that was the most enjoyable thing for me, because I got to choose someone I was interested in and study him. Now, it may just be because I like this sort of thing personally, but I think other people at LEAST enjoyed that part. The time frame was very nice, especially with that week off—that was REALLY nice. We had plenty of time, and I felt no rush at all. The actual assignment didn't take as long as I thought it would and I was REALLY thrilled when I was reading *Paradise Lost* and found the ACTUAL spot that Faulkner made a reference to. I think that was a really cool thing and that one moment made the whole thing worthwhile. Overall I wouldn't be opposed to doing it again. We had relatively little hard work to do during the period when we were writing the paper which was wonderful and it was probably the funnest project I have ever done.

The idea of having a student who reads *Paradise Lost* for pleasure and still writes "funnest" is the kind of thing that will keep me in the classroom forever. It is at such moments that I know the student has gone beyond any standard the state or I would ever construct and has truly achieved excellence.

Kjerstin Barret wrote her paper on Arthur Conan Doyle.

I thought the term paper was okay, not too bad. The only thing was that I procrastinated too long and had to do practically the whole thing over that week off in February. Another problem I had was the eye strain I got from the long hours I spent on the computer finding information. It was interesting though. At first I thought I was going to have a really hard time finding enough info to write five pages, then I found it hard to narrow it down to only eight. I also thought it was going to be really really hard to write, but I found that once I got all of my information and I started writing it just came naturally. It actually wasn't that bad, it just took a long time.

Trust me that Amos Goodman would use a formal tone for an informal note. That's Amos. He researched Paul Auster:

I thought that the research project was an excellent assignment. For me, and many others, it was our first chance at writing an essay of this length and caliber. It proved to be invaluable. Part of why this project was a success was the amount left up to us students. Since we were able not only to choose the subject, but the thesis as well, it was virtually impossible to not be interested. And interest leads to more research and enthusiasm, which created some wonderful papers.

I am all for the return of this project next year. I think it would be helpful to read more essays on novels we have read as a class, and then discuss the writer's point of view, and most importantly, the writer's skill in communication. Also, when the assignment is first assigned, remind students that they are all capable of writing a paper of this length, as several students in my class were contemplating a teacher change, to avoid this paper.

No one told me that he or she was contemplating a teacher change. The things you learn when you ask. With responses like these, I will most certainly be assigning literary research papers again next year. As for the year after that, I'll keep thinking and asking my students.

Researching Answers to Important Questions

I recently received a term paper from a student for whom I stretched the boundaries of the literary research assignment. Amanda is an avid reader who has faced enormous challenges in her sixteen years. She spent time in several foster homes and, though she has now returned to her mother and is living in a relatively stable environment, continues to puzzle over the relationships between adults and their children. She was struggling to find an author she cared enough about to research, so I suggested that instead she focus on books about youngsters who were forced by the absence of their parents to take responsibility for their own lives while still very young.

Within the next month Amanda read *Dangerous Angels* by Francesca Lia Block, *Girl* by Blake Nelson, *The Tribes of Palos Verdes* by Joy Nicholson, *Hideous Kinky* by Esther Freud, *Anywhere but Here* by Mona Simpson, *Bogeywoman* by Jaimy Gordon, *Stripping and Other Stories* by Pagan Kennedy, *Pamela: A Novel* by Pamela Yu, *Less Than Zero* by Bret Easton Ellis, *The Culture of Complaint* by Robert Hughes, *Tea* by Stacey D'Erasmo, and *A Tribe Apart* by Patricia Hersch. As Amanda told me in an e-mail message while struggling to formulate her thesis, "I know that some of these books are horribly written, Mrs. Jago, but they work for the idea."

Here is how Amanda's idea developed. Although as a teacher the last thing you are probably in the mood for is reading another term paper, I have reproduced Amada's paper here in its entirety to allow you to see the depth of this student's involvement with her subject. Isn't this the key to authentic research?

When Worlds Decline

"David Cassidy, he's just so dreamy!!!" It has been argued that teenagers have always resided in their own subdivision of culture, perhaps their own planet in particularly unfortunate cases. Statistics document the dark side of teenage culture, ranging from reports on teen drug use to pregnancy to violence. Adults absorb the numbers, reports, and horror stories through media in varied forms such as the news, Internet, or books. There is an adult populace that responds to these documents of teenage life as Pete Goslow, age thirty-two, responded to the novel *Less Than Zero* by Bret Easton Ellis: "It's certainly not my generation anymore." To which the teenage rebuttal is: "Parents just don't understand." Thus the separation of teens from their parents and the general adult world is declared.

Sociologist/psychiatrist Patricia Hersch speculates that "today's kids have an abundance of the 'space' the sixties kids coveted. It creates a milieu for growing up that adults cannot understand because their absence causes it" in her book, *A Tribe Apart*. The generation gap or lack of understanding created by absent parents Hersch writes of is beyond, as one amazon.com reader wrote in a review of the book, "parents not knowing what their kids do." It becomes pertinent to the pressure and responsibility that kids of the nineties have forced upon them due to the absence of their parents. Although the amazon.com reader is most likely correct that parents of the sixties did not have full knowledge of their children's activities, the responsibilities designated to teens then were remarkably different from the responsibilities layered onto teens and adolescents of the nineties. Because the conflicts and qualities of a culture are often reflected in literature from the corresponding time period, the responsibility and pressure placed on teens in the nineties has been the topic of several current novels. The novels written by contemporary women authors in the nineties describing experiences of girls include the increased responsibility that they take on as a result of their parents being absent mentally or physically.

Regardless of whether one believes the heavy responsibility put on teens to be the consequence of the culture of the sixties, the fact is that the break in parent and child worlds has widened since the sixties, forcing greater responsibility onto teens. As a person who existed in the sixties when a portion of her generation was labeled "hippies," Claudia Fonda-Bonardi gave the characterization of a hippie as "one searching for meaning in life" whereas a dictionary of the word "hippie" reads "one who rejects conventional behavior or dress." The dictionary touches the surface of the ideals of the hippies while Claudia Fonda-Bonardi's definition explains the process behind them. The difficulties that children of hippie parents encountered as a result of one such system are described in the 1960s-set novel *Hideous Kinky*. The blurb at the back of the novel describes the mother in the story as a hippie, her personifying the definition in saying, "I had plenty of good discipline and it didn't do me any good." The mother found discipline useless, frivolous and rejected the conventional idea of disciplining children. Thus, she rejects conventional ideas and is searching for a more meaningful substitute. However, when this tactic is repeated by many people in a small range of time, a universal change in the style of child upbringing that occurs in the affected areas is created. Perhaps when this change occurred around the sixties, children were given more freedom and with more freedom comes more responsibility. In the sixties, the responsibilities appear somewhat optional in comparison to the nineties. In *Hideous Kinky*, the mother cries over the departure of her friends and her youngest daughter "offered a song to cheer Mum up, but she was unenthusiastic for once." The daughter chooses to attempt to console her mother.

In the nineties, it becomes required that children console their parents, forcing responsibility for their parents onto children. Written in 1999, *Last Things* by Jenny Offill provides insight into the life of a young girl growing up with a parent requiring emotional support. At one point in the novel, the child is "belted inside the car before I [she] knew what was happening. My mother pointed out all the men she might have married. I grew tired of this game and began to sing. She put her hand over my mouth." Without choice, the child is placed in the presence of her grieving mother. Upon trying to mentally escape her mother's belittling comments about her father by way of singing, the mother prevents the protective mannerism of escape from occurring. This situation forces the child to please the parent by being with them when needed but also by forfeiting the child's own emotional outlet for the sake of letting the parent feel like someone is listening to their thoughts. Essentially the child is compelled into a position which requires that they listen to their parents vent their emotions, a responsibility totally inappropriate for a child, who by definition is "immature." It is true that the mother in *Last Things* is in a time of crisis but she could have found a more mature way of dealing with the situation, one that uses more emotional control, sadly demonstrated by the daughter who chooses to sing as opposed to have a tantrum.

The mother's tantrums and loss of control become almost constant in *Last Things* and as a result, she begins to expect this behavior out of her mother. The situation of a child providing parental support is further complicated when the parent's need for support is both extreme and capricious. In *Tea* by Stacey D'Erasmo, the mother's bouts of depression seem to appear from out of nowhere and are relatively potent. During the opening pages of *Tea*, the mother is talking about buying a house and announces to her daughter: "'Sometimes I want to die.' 'I [daughter] don't know what you're talking about. You drove us here. You'll drive us back.'" The child, somewhat stunned by the quick subject change, attempts to rationalize with her mother. Because the outburst occurs somewhat randomly, the child cannot elect to avoid being present when her mother will slip into sudden depression. In this particular scenario, it is obvious to the uninvolved observer that the mother needs to seek professional psychiatric help. However, the child, faced with the conflicts that a professional should handle is forced into the responsibility of trying to bring her mother out of her depression with the hope that her mother will not commit suicide. Additional responsibility is heaped onto the child in this situation should the parent commit suicide because there would be a sufficient amount of guilt that the child would attribute to itself for not bringing the parent out of the depression in order to prevent the death altogether. At the same time, the child, with parent either dead or alive, would also need to find a way to explain what happens when their parent falls into a depression to themselves.

These responsibilities are not the only responsibilities shoved into teens of the nineties. The mothers in both *Tea* and *Last Things* are mentally absent and are unaware of the responsibility they place onto their children. Both mothers become physically absent to their children by the end of each novel: in *Tea* by way of suicide, in *Last Things* by way of suspected suicide. In current literature, there is a prominence of death, divorce, or other means that leave a child with either one or no parents, a reflection of the thirty-two percent rate of children living with one or without either parent (US Census Bureau). Even in the kitsch *Dangerous Angels*, a compilation of the "modern day fairy tales" (amazon.com) of Francesca Lia Block, there is death, neglect, and divorce. In the first story of *Dangerous Angels*, entitled *Weetzie Bat*, the protagonist asks her parents the reason for their divorce to which they responded: "Your mother turned bitter, like . . . well what's the bitterest thing?" and her mother calling her father "a lush." The accusations of each parent are heard by the daughter, yet she doesn't react harshly, showing an air of maturity, even in her late teens/early adulthood. The rationale for the mellow reaction of the protagonist may be such maturity. However, Block is said to "believe in the healing power of love" (qtd. in *The Book Bag*). This belief may have been applied to the protagonist of *Weetzie Bat*, meaning that because both parents have loved her and she has loved them, the force of love would outweigh the accusations and render them unbelievable to her. The child is still expected to be able to tolerate listening to her parents call each other names, which is a childish way for the parents to assign blame. In any case, there are children who do not have access to love and support that they would need to recover from the blows they receive from their parents' dysfunction and what they have been shown repeatedly to be normal.

It is a large task for a person to overcome a dysfunctional child-hood, the first problem being that the child needs to recognize that their childhood was dysfunctional. By pushing the responsi-bility for parental emotions onto kids, a pattern is created chang-ing the way children are raised. Children were not put on earth to take care of their parents' problems. They are not their parents' therapists. They are children; synonymous with the word "imma-ture" because they are in a state of perpetual learning, parents being the first teachers they encounter. Supposedly, when chil-dren mature, they are called "adults." Children should not be expected to pat an adult on the back because they are suicidal at the moment and then give them a therapy session on the spot. Yet children try. The fact that they do so shows that the children of the nineties may not be the lazy, irresponsible generation that they are often labeled. Perhaps the responsibilities and the split between parents and kids began in the sixties with the choice to discipline less, perhaps not. Any which way one believes the fissure between teens and parents to have been spawned: there is a problem. A growing problem. At this point in time, it is not all adults that put these responsibilities onto their children, but dysfunction spreads. When responsibility is placed on a child to deal with their parents' outbursts, tantrums, suicidal inklings, etc. the child is given the example that children are supposed to take responsibility for their parents. Then, the children will recreate the situation when they have children because it is what they have been taught is the standard procedure for raising children. Also, those who experience dysfunctional childhoods will often recreate the situation in their romantic involvements, spreading dysfunction to those that they are linked to. Thus the number of dysfunctional adults becomes larger and the number of functional adults smaller. In the U.S., in the nineties, we have a situation of dysfunction breeding dysfunction. The culture of the future may be completely dysfunctional, each person being unable to support themselves or each other, a dysfunctional world. It's a man-made epidemic, spreading like a disease, the result of the decline of the mentally functional world.

By Amanda Allan

While Amanda at age fifteen clearly still has work to do in order to communicate her ideas clearly, this is a student who has blown the top off any research standard. In pursuit of answers to her own real questions, Amanda turned to books. As a result, she achieved a level of excellence both in terms of research and in terms of her reading that goes far beyond anything policymakers could ever imagine setting as a standard.

Six

Beyond Literature Standards

*W*hat is disconcerting about most states' standards for high school literature study is that they are both too easy and too hard. That is, for some students the standards fall far short of the kind of work they are capable of, while for others the standards describe levels of achievement far beyond their ability. Take, for example, Learning Standard 17, from the Massachusetts English Language Arts Standards document (1997): "Students will interpret the meaning of literary works, nonfiction, films, and media by using different critical lenses and analytic techniques" (50). This standard applies to students in grades four through twelve.

By the twelfth grade, Massachusetts students are expected to be able to "Analyze the moral and philosophical arguments presented in novels, films, plays, essays, or poems; an author's political ideology, as portrayed in a selected work, or collections of works, or archetypal patterns found in works of literature and nonfiction" (50). I wonder if there was a senior English teacher among the group that wrote this sentence. Somehow I doubt it.

The Tricky Business of Literature Standards

Without underestimating what students are capable of accomplishing, I think it is fair to say that the average high school senior would find it very difficult to meet Massachusetts' standard. We don't expect every student to make the varsity soccer team or to qualify to join a madrigal group. We don't hold up the performance of orchestra members as a standard for musical achievement for all students, so why should we set such an unrealistic standard for students' literary understanding? Of course teachers should hold lofty goals like the one this Massachusetts standard describes as we design curricula that will challenge and inspire students, but to expect every one of our charges to be able to analyze archetypal patterns is absurd.

The California language arts document includes high school standards so out of touch with classroom reality that English teachers who read them will feel they have drunk from Alice in Wonderland's magical bottle. "Students will analyze the philosophical arguments presented in literary works, determining whether the author's position has contributed to the quality of the work and the believability of the characters" (1997, 68). One may as well set a standard that every senior will write a novel before graduation. Benchmarks like this don't improve education. They only make teachers whose students will never meet them fear that an angry Queen of Hearts will burst into the teachers' lunchroom and begin to shout, "Off with their heads!"

Teachers should be held accountable for student performance, but there is no simple formula for equating teaching with learning. All I have to do to illustrate the problem is compare two of my own classes.

By spring in my honors class, all but three or four students have made significant gains in reading since September. These teenagers have read eight books, written six essays, and taken part in daily class discussions about literature. As a result, I can demonstrate with papers from their portfolios that their writing has improved dramatically. Although we have no comparative test scores for these students, I believe that their ability to read challenging texts has also increased. They have certainly had plenty of practice.

During this same interval in my regular English class, all but three or four students have made little progress. Those few students who have aren't necessarily smarter than the rest, nor were they privy to a magic formula for pleasing Mrs. Jago. They simply paid attention in class, completed their homework, studied for tests, and read the assigned books. The others did not.

Rating my performance as a teacher on the basis of student growth from the honors class would make me look like a superteacher. Using the regular class as a measure would make me seem barely adequate. Same teacher, different results. Not all low student test scores are the product of poor instruction.

If teachers are to be held accountable, and I believe they should be, so must others. School principals must be held accountable for providing a safe environment for teaching and learning. They need to find alternatives for disruptive students so that those who want to learn are able to work. They must also keep administrivial distractions to a minimum and consider classroom time sacred.

Students must be held accountable, too. Though many by necessity work in the evening to support their families and have limited time for schoolwork after three P.M., too many waste the hours they have. Every day I see students doing anything but what their teacher has asked: flipping through *Bride* magazine, writing notes, chucking sticks of gum across the room, staring off into space. This behavior is rarely seen in an honors class.

I accept responsibility for students who do not engage as I would hope, and I continue to try the best I can to find ways to motivate them. What I refuse to do is turn my lessons into games and pretend that learning does not require determined student effort.

Many who return from the wonderland of college tell me they have been well prepared. But like Alice, I feel a bit lost. I know I set high standards in my own classroom and, at least for fifty-five minutes at a time, am able to persuade students to follow me down the rabbit hole to learning. I am simply unconvinced that state standards will help me do this better.

"What sort of people live about here?"

"In that direction," the Cat said, waving its right paw round, "lives a Hatter: and in that direction," waving the other paw, "lives a March Hare. Visit either you like: they're both mad."

"But I don't want to go among mad people," Alice remarked.

"Oh, you can't help that," said the Cat: "we're all mad here. I'm mad. You're mad."

"How do you know I'm mad?" said Alice.

"You must be," said the Cat, "or you wouldn't have come here."

So that's why I remain in education. Leave it to the Cheshire Cat to explain.

Literature: The Business of Madmen and Heretics

Upon leaving Russia in 1920, Yevgeny Zamyatin wrote that "True literature only exists when it is created by madmen, hermits, heretics, dreamers, rebels, and skeptics; not by reliable clerks just doing their jobs" (Radzinskii 1997). One has only to think of some of our own country's literary giants—Poe, Twain, Hemingway, Morrison—to be persuaded by Zamyatin's argument. I wonder, then, why English teachers so often treat works of genius like corpses to be dissected. Maybe it is because we see ourselves as reliable clerks just doing our jobs.

What is the job of an English teacher, anyway? Is it to take a list of literary terms and teach students how to spot metaphors and imagery, alliteration and allegory? Is it to lecture teenagers on the difference between a romantic reading of a text and a Marxist-feminist reading? If I thought that, I would quit tomorrow. While teachers don't have the professional latitude to be madmen or heretics, skepticism is as positive a virtue in a teacher as is a gift for dreaming. Call me a dreamer, but I believe an English teacher's job is to help students become thoughtful readers.

Thoughtful reading requires discipline as well as structure, which is where the teaching of literary terminology comes in. Terms should help students better understand what they have read, not create barriers to passing the class. My students find it easier to talk about poetry when they have such words as *metaphor* and *imagery* in their vocabulary. Just as a carpenter would be frustrated trying to build a shelf without tools, students who haven't learned literary terms often struggle when they write about literature.

An Australian high school teacher, Brian Moon, has written a book called *Literary Terms: A Practical Glossary* (1999) that offers ideas about how to make the shift from teaching terms for the sake of identification to teaching literary concepts as tools for thoughtful reading. Instead of viewing literature as a body of objective knowledge to be mastered, Moon considers it a field of social practice within which readers and writers act. His redefinition works for me.

In the chapter on imagery, for example, Moon quotes Samuel Taylor Coleridge from *The Rime of the Ancient Mariner*. The questions that follow do not ask students to identify the imagery, but instead invite them to think about whether the mental pictures Coleridge's words create have been generated by the words themselves or by a combination of the words and the reader's own experiences and memories. Moon then asks whether anyone can ever be sure that the images he or she "sees" are the same as the ones another reader sees. This is the kind of teaching that helps students become thoughtful readers. It also avoids the dissection model of literary analysis.

Even Yevgeny Zamyatin, who declared literature the province of madmen and heretics, believed in the use of literary terminology as a vehicle for talking about what we see when we read. Identifying himself as a neorealist, Zamyatin explained, "While neorealism uses a microscope to look at the world, symbolism uses a telescope. Pre-revolutionary realists, on the other hand, employ an ordinary looking glass." Even to someone who has never read a word by Zamyatin, his comparison offers a picture of the kind of fictional world a reader might expect to find in one of his novels. It comes as no surprise that, in painting this picture for us, the writer resorted to imagery.

The Goldilocks Assignment

You might think that after twenty-five years in the classroom I would have figured out how to begin a poetry unit. I certainly would have expected it. Instead, I find myself ever on the lookout for new ways to introduce this genre. Poems can bring such pleasure to teenagers if I can only find a way to get around their initial fear and loathing.

Sitting at an English teachers conference listening to my own former Milton professor describe an assignment he used to begin a class on poetry at the University of California at Santa Barbara, I had an idea. Sheridan Blau called his project "The Goldilocks Assignment." The steps were simple. Students had to choose three poems—one that was too easy, one that was too hard, and one that was just right—then present the poems to their classmates. What I instinctively liked about the assignment was that it began with readers and books. Instead of my standing on stage offering a captive audience poems I liked in order to persuade others that they might like them, too, students had to do the persuading. I also loved the idea that these young people would be reading many, many poems in order to find one that was "just right."

One thing I have learned over the years is that high school students need even elegantly simple assignments like this one to be broken down into a series of steps. The English majors in Dr. Blau's course could go off to the library and find what they needed for the next class meeting, then come in and companionably share their findings. My students would need a plan of action. I also knew that I was going to need to hold them accountable for documenting their search with a finished product. With thirty-seven students in the room, I would never be able to listen in on their small groups enough to establish that each and every student had actually done what the assignment demanded. They were going to have to write a paper.

I began with a chart. In my experience, teachers expend a great deal of effort creating beautiful assignment sheets that students toss the minute they leave the room. By posting an assignment, I give students a visual aid to refer to throughout their work. Any students who wish to copy the assignment (with some classes I make them do this) will have the added benefit of actually having their eyes consciously focus on every word. This method also saves time at the photocopier, as well as trees.

The Goldilocks Assignment

Your challenge: To find three poems

- one that is "too easy"
- one that is "too hard"
- one that is "just right"

Your paper: Write an essay in which you present all three poems, explaining why you categorized each as you have. **Due:** _____

Your presentation: In a 5-minute oral presentation, read your "just right" poem to the class telling us why this poem was just right for you. Sign up for a time slot and please do not let us down by being absent on that day.

Initially students are frustrated. "I don't know any poems, Mrs. Jago. Where are we supposed to find them?" On cue, I bring out boxes of books—individual volumes of poetry as well as single copies of every anthology I can find in the school's book room. I check out as many books by single authors as the school and public libraries will let me take and supplement them with books from home. I put out everything from collections of cowboy poetry to the complete works of Langston Hughes, from Shel Silverstein to William Blake, from Billy Collins to Christina Rossetti. I also do not display the books in any particular order. I invite students to let poems find them, to pick up books almost at random, drawn by a cover or a quirky title, and then to graze through the selections looking for poems that for whatever reason strike them.

It is a messy and sometimes noisy process. Students are excited to show others what they have found, sometimes for reasons of beauty, sometimes for shock value. As they are reading, we always stop and talk about contemporary poets' use of graphic language. I tell students that if they see a poem that offends them to turn the page or put down the book. There are plenty of others to choose from. This seldom stops the class clown from passing around a poem full of four-letter words, but it does limit the reaction he gets from others. (Sorry to seem sexist here, but it is always a "he.")

Because students must include copies of the poems in their essays, a great deal of copying takes place. To me, copying out poems is an act of love. I never fail to understand a poem a bit better after typing it up. If students seem to be avoiding long poems because they don't want to copy out pages worth of poetry, I tell them to photocopy the poem, and they simply attach it to their paper. In their hunt for three poems, students read pages and pages of poetry, much more than I could ever assign. They never see how I have tricked them into doing so much reading. Every student comes away from the assignment with a poem identified as "just right." Like Goldilocks, kids know what they like.

Many students have never actually seen poetry in individual volumes by a single author before. The only way that they know poetry lives in the world is inside heavy literature anthologies surrounded by colorful artwork and followed by a series of questions about theme and narrative voice. As they pick up *Love Poems* by Nikki Giovanni, *Loose Woman* by Sandra Cisneros, or *The Concrete River* by Luis Rodriguez, students begin to discover how reading a series of poems by the same writer can be a window into the inner life of another human being. It never surprises me to see students choose writers who look like them, or how often the "just right" poems come from these books.

I want to open students up to the joy and solace poems can offer. As the following student papers demonstrate, the Goldilocks assignment seemed to help teenagers achieve that goal. Do these essays meet state standards? Have these students demonstrated that they can "evaluate the aesthetic qualities of style, including the impact of diction and figurative language on tone, mood, and theme, using the terminology of literary criticism" (*English-Language Arts Content Standards for California Public Schools,* 58)? I think they do.

Yazmin Sandoval is an English language learner enrolled in her first class outside the ESL program. While she does not use the terminology of literary criticism, her heartfelt response to what she reads tells me she is well on her way to meeting California's standard for literary criticism. Yazmin's Goldilocks essay demonstrates a deep understanding of the poems and of herself as a reader of poetry. She followed the instructions with precision. Though she is reluctant to take part in class discussions under normal circumstances, Yazmin—though nervous—presented her "just right" poem to the class with poise.

> To classify a poem as too easy, too hard, and just right is a difficult task to complete. Each person has different methods of approaching a poem because each individual has distinct preferences. I can only speak for myself. When I read a poem I create a world of my own. The world I create in my mind may not be the same as the one that the writer was thinking about at the time of writing the poem. It is this effect that poems create that make them so unique and adventurous.
>
> I found "That Day," a poem by Nikki Giovanni, to be very easy. I enjoyed the poem when I read it, but I found it to be very straight forward. Just by reading it, I knew what the poem was about or at least what I was imagining it to be about. I felt the poem did not even give me an opportunity to create a meaning of my own and it was this that made it too easy for me.
>
> A poem that was too hard for me was "Song on Beholding an Enlightenment" by Matias de Bocanegra. As much as I tried to read the poem, it seemed I could not finish it because some of the words it included were too difficult and I did not know their meaning. I would go to the dictionary every time I saw something unfamiliar, but I realized after a while that I had no idea of what the poem was even about. It was just not possible for me to feel what the writer was feeling at the moment of writing the poem.
>
> A poem that was just right for me was "Romance of the Living Corpse" by Enrique Gonzalez Martinez. The vocabulary in the poem was not too difficult. The poem allowed me to use my

imagination as I read it and make of it as I desired at the moment. I was also able to appreciate the poem even more because of my own recent love life and my attraction to romantic poems.

I don't exactly know why this happens, but I always have a few students in any class who seem to feel perfectly free to ignore the dictates of an assignment and write what they like. Jeff Weston decided that instead of writing about "too hard" or "too easy" poems, he would simply write about three poems that were "just right." What I like about what he has done here is that he offers a rationale for this decision.

What makes a poem easy? How can a poem be too easy? Is it so easy that it cannot have more meaning than it obviously states? Is it short? When is a poem too hard? Is it too hard when I cannot understand it? For what is it too hard? For comprehension? For enjoyment? Is a poem too hard when I can understand and interpret fairly well what the author is saying yet am overloaded by too much, too many symbols, too much meaning? Can something ever have too much meaning? I do not know. I do not know if I will ever know.

What I do know is that certain poems are just right. They have meaning at the time I read them. They stick in my mind, for a while at least. Therefore, instead of choosing a too easy, too hard, and just right poem, I have chosen to write about three "just right" poems.

I love Carl Sandburg's "Fog." I actually read it the first time in fifth grade. Fog is compared to a cat. Like a cat, the fog is stealthy and creeps on "silent haunches." There is symbolism yet the author keeps it simple—fog is like a cat. I have never analyzed the poem thoroughly. I just know that I like it, especially the ending. It builds up toward line four but then calms back down closing with a short, four-syllable line.

I also like Langston Hughes' poem "Island." It is simple and speaks of longing for a better life. The tone is sorrowful. Anyone can relate to this poem because it expresses the classic grass-is-always-greener idea. Finally, I like John Taggart's "Against the Nurses of Experience." Like all of the Taggart poems I read in *Loop*, it has a free form. Not held back by punctuation, the words flow. The author uses balance, changing the order of the words to achieve a circular effect.

Jeff's essay clearly meets the English Language Arts (ELA) standard in terms of employing literary terminology in his analysis, yet I think his bold decision to write only about poems that were just right for him demonstrates how he has exceeded the standard. Jeff has the intellectual confidence to reshape an assignment to meet his own learning needs. Isn't that what we want all students to possess?

Abby Gordon didn't need a classroom assignment to turn her on to poetry. What the Goldilocks assignment did was provide her with the opportunity to examine her own enthusiasm for poetry through an analytic lens.

Right now I am the Goldilocks of poetry, eating up poems, and picking some that are "too hard," "too easy," and "just right." Although I can choose these poems somewhat easily, I also must examine why some of these poems just don't taste right, why some of them I would rather just leave in a book somewhere and never pick up again while others ring with a unique sense of beauty in my mind. Why do I duplicate these poems, hang them on my wall, send them to friends in greeting cards, illustrate them . . . love them beyond belief?

"Too hard," I assign to a poem called "Bavarian Gentians." Even after reading it twice, and typing it up, I have no idea of what it is about. I don't really have any clue as to what a "Bavarian Gentian" is. Maybe it was something everyone knew in 1932 when D. H. Lawrence wrote the poem, but I am not living in 1932, and I definitely don't know what a Bavarian Gentian is, thus making it extremely difficult for me to put any form of meaning behind the poem. The poem just doesn't ring in my ears. There are too many titles, and mystical names that I am not familiar with. Due to the fact that I am unfamiliar with many of the names and concepts in this poem, it is very hard for me to read. I stumble over words and question myself as to where one phrase begins and where another ends. I feel silly trying to put emotion into this reading because I don't know what I feel about the poem. Acknowledging that I do not feel anything toward the poem except annoyance, I realize that some poetry is not for me, and I think that this is one of those poems.

I love Shel Silverstein. I've read many of his books, laughing and smiling as I do, and find myself talking in rhymes after reading one of his poetry books from cover to cover. I love the way that many of his poems make me smile, while others remind me of the creativity in the world. While I love Silverstein's work, I think that the poems are not really meant for me. While they make me smile, they are just a quick fix, and I don't find myself really thinking about them. The reason for this is because these poems are for children. Silverstein can't talk about love, or sex, or rage. He can't say, "Fuck you" or describe the beauty of seduction. His poems exclude a plethora of ideas and thoughts which makes me feel they are limited. While I very much enjoy Silverstein's work, it is not something that I would have read at my wedding.

A perfect poem . . . that's hard to find. Maybe there isn't such a thing. A perfect poem to me is generally not going to be a perfect poem to others. I like the way that poems can evoke emotion. The way that even though the author might be writing about something completely different, I am able to feel, and believe in the poem for more personal reasons. In the poem "The Road Not Taken" by Robert Frost, he is talking about a trail that he has chosen. Talking about the decision he made to take one path rather than another. While talking about a road, there is more in this poem. There are metaphors and allusions to my life. I say "my life" because when given a poem with such girth, it can be an individual experience. I can believe that the things I feel from this poem are exclusively for me. I love that. I love being able to feel a poem, to be able to experience it within myself. To be able to read it, not stumbling over words and phrases, but having them flow from me in a calm rhythm that is pleasing to my ears. I experience the meaning of the poem individually.

In all the years I have taught Robert Frost, I have never found a term so perfect as Abby's "girth" for describing what "The Road Not Taken" offers readers. Of the few things I know for sure, one is that students have much to teach me.

When Students Do the Teaching

Last April I was struggling with a class of seniors who could not keep their minds on their schoolwork. College admissions officers had made their decisions, and the long-awaited envelopes began arriving. Even the most dutiful of students had trouble focusing on anything but the drama playing out in their mailboxes. Students pretended to listen, but you could feel their minds were elsewhere. How did she get in when I didn't? Should I go to UCLA or the University of Michigan? Why did Berkeley say yes while Boston College said no? Who is going to pay for all this? Am I ready to leave home? I should be happy. Why aren't I?

The only thing I could think of to get my students' minds off college and back on the curriculum was to celebrate National Poetry Month. I also knew I still had quite a lot of work left to do with this group to prepare them for the AP literature exam. Celebrating National Poetry Month seemed a perfect way to marry pleasure with duty. Dividing students into small groups, I assigned each group a poet to research and present to the class. Their instructions were to teach us about Wallace Stevens, Federico Garcia Lorca, Gertrude Stein, Rainer Maria Rilke, e. e. cummings, and others, but also to lead a discussion of poems by these writers.

Questioning the Author

We had been working on a technique for developing discussion questions that borrowed from Isabel Beck's "questioning the author" research. Instead of "gotcha" questions that simply assess student comprehension after reading, Beck's "queries" assist students as they grapple with text to construct meaning. Given that students were going to be teaching extremely sophisticated and difficult poetry to their peers, it seemed an ideal moment to hone all of our skills at asking questions that encouraged further exploration of the text.

In order to emphasize the difference between traditional discussion questions and queries, we made a list on the board of typical teacherly questions for Thomas Hardy's "The Convergence of the Twain." (I was hoping the *Titanic* connection might wake students up a bit, too.)

The Convergence of the Twain
(Lines on the loss of the 'Titanic')

I
In a solitude of the sea
Deep from human vanity,
And the Pride of Life that planned her, stilly couches she.
II
Steel chambers, late the pyres
Of her salamandrine fires,
Cold currents thrid, and turn to rhythmic tidal lyres.
III
Over the mirrors meant
To glass the opulent
The sea-worm crawls—grotesque, slimed, dumb, indifferent.
IV
Jewels in joy designed
To ravish the sensuous mind
Lie lightless, all their sparkles bleared and black and blind.
V
Dim moon-eyed fishes near
Gaze at the gilded gear
And query: "What does this vaingloriousness down here?"
VI
Well: while was fashioning
This creature of cleaving wing,
The Immanent Will that stirs and urges everything
VII
Prepared a sinister mate
For her—so gaily great—
A Shape of Ice, for the time far and dissociate.

VIII

And as the smart ship grew
In stature, grace, and hue,
In shadowy silent distance grew the Iceberg too.

IX

Alien they seemed to be:
No mortal eye could see
The intimate welding of their later history,

X

Or sign that they were bent
By paths coincident
On being anon twin halves of one august event

XI

Till the Spinner of the Years
Said "Now!" And each one hears,
And consummation comes, and jars two hemispheres.

Thomas Hardy

Students came up with

- What is the theme of this poem?
- What does the iceberg symbolize?
- Explain how the form matches the poem's message.
- What literary device does Hardy employ in the line "Jewels in joy designed"?
- Who is the "Spinner of the Years"?

I then offered students an alternative list of queries, and we talked about how these questions might encourage a different kind of discussion about the Hardy poem:

- What is the poet trying to say here?
- What is the poet's message?
- What does the poet mean when he says _____?
- How does this poem connect with what you know about the *Titanic*?
- Has the poem changed your thinking about the sinking of the *Titanic* in any way?

Students were able to see immediately how much more interesting it would be to respond to these kinds of questions. I then asked them to, along with researching the poet's life and work, construct a handful of queries for their presentation. I also told them not to worry if they never got around to posing these queries. Our discussion might have a momentum of its own and cover these ideas without their ever having been raised.

Courtney Cazden has said that "It is easy to imagine talk in which ideas are explored rather than answers to teachers' test questions provided and evaluated . . . Easy to imagine, but not easy to do" (1988). I am constantly looking for ways to encourage authentic classroom discussion, the kind where students actually talk about the things in a poem that they care about rather than the things I have determined they should care about. It's a delicate balance to strike.

The Rilke group got everyone's attention when they explained that poor Rainer's mother dressed him as a girl, but I felt students were still only half paying attention. It wasn't so much the poor quality of the questions that were being posed but the white noise inside students' heads I sensed. They simply could not focus on anything outside themselves. Then Elina Segal read Imamu Amiri Baraka's poem "Air." This deceptively simple series of images about loss seemed to float off the page, just as I think many in the room wished their own worries might lift from their shoulders. For no clear reason other than the voodoo that a particular poem can sometimes work on particular readers at a particular moment, the class came alive. It was such a relief to have students once again jabbering about what they thought the poem meant that I could have cheered.

ELINA: So what do you think this poet is trying to do here?

TAYLOR: I think he's made the poem really skinny with only a couple or sometimes one word on a line to make it light, like air.

ANDREA: Yeah, he even shortens words like "w/" and uses "&" instead of "and" so that even the few words he puts on the page are as weightless as possible.

ELINA: But why?

ANDREA: Well, the poet says that he's trying to get out of something so maybe the whole poem is a way of floating away from a bad situation or problem or something.

TAYLOR: That's what I see, too, only I don't understand the line where he says "you / are the weakness / of my simplicity." What does that mean, Elina?

ELINA: I don't know. Anybody got any ideas?

The bell rang to end class before they exhausted Elina's query.

The next day, Rachel Rosemarin, Jessica Perez, and Devon Pollard read D. H. Lawrence's "Piano" and explained how listening to a song triggered a series of powerful memories of the poet's mother. "Taking me back down the vista of years, till I see / A child sitting under the piano, in the boom of the tingling strings / and pressing the small, poised feet of a mother who smiles as she sings." We talked about how memories are triggered and then Devon asked the class to write poems of our own that began with a recent memory. In the few minutes he gave us, I thought about last weekend when I was taken out on San Francisco Bay for the first time.

> Night sail on the bay
> I know nothing about boats
> Or water, or rigging
> No knot I tie holds
> Can't steer by the stars
> Let alone by heart.

When Devon asked who would like to read my hand shot up. It's a lovely feeling to write something you like and share it with those you love. I guess I needed to get my mind off worrying about these seniors as much as they needed to stop worrying about themselves. Reading and writing poetry was exactly the antidote we needed. This became particularly apparent on the last day of presentations, when Carmelle offered the class Elizabeth Bishop's "Sestina" and then invited us to write a sestina of our own. Students, particularly the mathematicians in a class, love the rigorous demands of this form. As I'm sure you remember, a sestina has six unrhymed stanzas of six lines each in which the words at the ends of the first stanza's lines recur in a rolling pattern at the ends of all the other lines. The poem concludes with a tercet that also uses all six end-words, two per line.

Niani Morse took up the challenge and used the form to confront the questions that I knew were in so many of these students' hearts. She had just been accepted at Pacific University in Oregon and was going to be leaving a boyfriend behind in Los Angeles.

Sestina

March rain brings relief
From draught, from dust,
From distraction of the semester last,
Of my last year in high school.
I stay in bed and listen to the rain
And read books I've wanted to for so long.

I've been with the same people for too long,
The change will bring relief.
Good-bye California dust.
My mom will pack me up and sigh and say, "At last!"
And I will move off to a new school,
In the rain.

Everyone but me is bothered by the rain
They say the winters are wet and long,
And I say the change from smoggy LA will be a relief.
All my 18 winters have been filled with Santa Ana's heat and
    dust.

Winter will come at last
And then there is the school.

Who knows what to expect from such a school,
In a new state known primarily for its rain,
Coming from a state known primarily for its summers so
    long?
Will this really bring relief?
What if I change my mind and like the dust?
What if the novelty of college doesn't last?

Love that lasts
Through the first year of a new school,
In the rain,
Is not long.
This thought will not bring him relief,
When he must remain here, without me, in the dust.

Left in my dust,
He will ask me if we will last
When I go away to school,
And if I will call him when it rains.
September will be long
For him, and his heart will feel little relief.

I have waited for so long to dust off my suitcase,
And pack up, and head out to that school in the rain.
At last I have the chance, and don't feel the relief I always
    imagined.

Though no questions about sestinas appeared on the AP
exam that Niani sat for, I believe she left class prepared—
prepared not only for multiple-choice questions about poetic
forms but also for leaving home.

Seven

Beyond Assessment Standards

In Jean-Paul Sartre's play *No Exit*, three newly dead characters are condemned for eternity to one another's company. "You remember all we were told about the torture-chambers, the fire and brimstone, the burning marl. Old wives' tales! There's no need for red-hot pokers. Hell is—other people!" Considering the number of teenagers who are likely to flunk the various high school exit exams that have been put in place across the country, I wonder if we are about to see a case of life imitating art. On the one hand, I believe that we must find new ways of assessing student achievement that measure excellence rather than simply benchmark skills. At the same time, teachers must recognize that before students can go beyond standardized assessments, they need to go through them.

Exit Exams

Governor Gray Davis vowed that California's exit exam would be "second to none in America." He said that his goal was to gauge students in a way that would stretch them. It is hard to argue with the man's good intentions. We all want a high school diploma to mean more than classroom seat time. But what will it be like to teach in a school where only a handful of seniors are allowed to walk across the stage in June? Who will answer angry parents when they demand to know how this happened? Imagine trying to run for office in a district where only 10 percent of the student body graduates. Orders for caps and gowns are likely to be way down.

If we don't want this hellish scenario played out, schools are going to have to act. It's not as though we don't know which students are in danger of not passing the dread exam. All a school has to do is look at last year's standardized test results and this year's grades. Any eighth grader with test scores in the bottom quartile in reading or math and with less than a C average is on target to fail the exit exam. It doesn't take a psychometrician to figure this out. All it takes is common sense and the willingness to look bad news in the eye.

So what's to be done? Every parent of an eighth grader who fits this profile should receive a letter from the school inviting him or her to a meeting where options for an accelerated learning program are laid out. Parents should be able to choose from Saturday school, summer school, or after-school programs. If they or their children choose none of the above, parents and students should be counseled about the consequences of leaving school without a high school diploma.

As students enroll in these acceleration programs, they must commit to more than simple attendance. It might help to teach students the Latin root *attendere*, "to stretch toward and give heed to." Teachers and tutors are going to have to inspire these young people to want the learning that has, for whatever reason, gotten past them up to now.

If Americans want a graduation requirement that promotes rather than discourages academic achievement, we are going to have to ensure that all students have a fair shot at passing exit exams. As Stanley Rabinowitz of WestEd, an education consulting group in San Francisco, has said, "Setting the high scores makes you feel good today, but that's not half of the battle. Do you have the fortitude to provide remediation and systemic accountability? Do you even know what to do?" (Olson 1999, 26).

Too many students already view high school in hellish terms. Installing "No Exit" signs without offering kids a reasonable chance to find their academic way out will only make things worse.

Playing the Game of School

How is it that some students seem to know instinctively how to get the best from their teachers while others invariably butt heads with every teacher they meet? I considered polling my colleagues to try to figure out the answer, but when I came across Devon's essay "How to Get an A When You Don't Deserve One," I realized that it is students, not teachers, who are the experts in this matter.

Devon's essay focused on an imaginary, hard-working friend who was not receiving top grades. Devon had determined to help him, though her assistance would not be in the form of tutoring, but in guidelines for manipulation. "Teachers know who they can and cannot get away with giving a B. If you are not careful, you end up in the B-receiving majority." The paper outlines a plan of action to make sure this never happens.

> I attended one of my friend's classes for a week and noted his every move. I spotted problem number one right away. He sat in the front row of the classroom. You see, teachers are much more apt to pay attention to and try to pull in the students who sit on the edges or in the back. The students that are in a constant battle with the teacher over attentiveness are the ones the teacher thinks about, gets to know, and therefore cares most about. Right away I moved my friend into the back-second-to-the corner seat. The teacher noticed immediately and wanted to talk with him about it.
>
> The next mistake my friend made was to ask questions constantly, thus getting them all answered during the class period. I explained that he should simply take notes, ask one question to show attentiveness (teachers do not differentiate between those who ask one or two questions and those who ask five or six) and then come in before or after school to get the rest of his questions answered. For just ten minutes of your time, you show the teacher that you are willing to go that extra mile. You also develop a

personal relationship with that teacher, making you one of her "special students." It also gives the teacher the illusion that you are trying your hardest even if you are not.

The next day was the test. I instructed my friend to be smart and study the night before, but I also advised him to follow my test taking strategies: 1) If you know and are sure of the answer then of course write it down. 2) If you are not sure that your answer is right, do the problem an alternative way and leave both answers. One of them will probably be nearly correct and she will at least give you partial credit. 3) If you don't know the answer at all, write down as much rubbish as you can and include a joke on the side of the paper. Most teachers will give you some credit for trying, and if not, your joke will give them a laugh, something most test papers won't. 4) Once the test is given back to you, check it carefully, looking for any mistakes the teacher may have made or any way to get extra points (i.e. I just accidentally wrote a + sign instead of x. I knew what I was doing though). The teacher may just give you those points when she isn't surrounded by 200 other tests.

Believe it or not, after all four steps had been completed, my friend had a 92% on his test—his best grade yet! We still had a long way to go, however. The next day I observed that my friend emitted a happy-go-lucky attitude whenever he entered the class. This I told him was a definite no-no. Teachers think that the tortured soul is the most intelligent one. Unhappy students attract sympathy and respect. Teachers, in turn, are more apt to grade easier, excuse late assignments and forgive absences for these "deep thinkers." That same day, my friend tried it out and burst out crying during class. The teacher saw his pain and let him have an extra day to turn in the homework.

Reading Devon's paper got me wondering. Am I really this transparent? Do students really have us wrapped around their little fingers? Fortunately a few stalwarts remain in the field. When my son complained that his answer to the chloroplast question was the same as Amir's and why did Amir get nine points while he got only eight, his science teacher took off a point for quibbling. Thank goodness somebody is out there still holding the line.

An amusing postscript to Devon's essay is that this expert on getting around teachers has begun teaching herself. When I showed her what she had written at age seventeen, Devon could only shake her head and smile.

Teacher, Test Thyself

The air inside the shabby classroom shimmered with tension. Both proctor and teenage test takers had far too much on their minds to notice the presence of an unlikely forty-something candidate sitting for this exam. I sharpened my pencils, set my watch on the desk the way I saw other students doing, and tried to focus on the droning instructions being read aloud. It wasn't easy.

The logic behind putting myself through this ordeal was to experience firsthand what sitting for the SAT II felt like for my students and to figure out how well my high school's curriculum matched the skills required for these high-stakes tests. As I mentioned in Chapter One, I had always in the past taken a rabid anti–test prep stance. I believed coursework in English should remain pure, focusing on literary analysis and the development of student writing. I was convinced that such instruction prepared my students for any qualifying exams they would ever have to face.

The SAT II subject tests that I sat for used to be known as Achievement Tests. They are hour-long, primarily multiple-choice tests in specific subjects. Unlike the SAT I, which measures general abilities, these tests measure students' knowledge of particular subjects and their ability to apply that knowledge. Many colleges, including the University of California, require that applicants submit scores for these tests, often including the writing exam. Most of the students I talked with in line outside the test center were juniors in high school taking three tests at one sitting, typically writing, mathematics, and chemistry or biology.

I am delighted to report that current high school curricula in writing, properly executed, prepare students extremely well for the portion of the writing exam in which they are actually asked to write. The questions are similar to the writing assignments students often face in school. The rubric used to evaluate the writing sample is congruent with those most teachers have been using for years. The biggest challenge for test takers is the length of time allotted—twenty minutes to plan and execute their essays.

The literature test is made up of five passages or poems. Students must read and answer multiple-choice questions based on each text. The literature was chosen from a broad range of authors and time periods. My exam included a passage from Bharatee Mukherjee's *Jasmine*, a portion of a Zora Neal Hurston essay, and a John Donne poem. Again, I think this reflects the blend of classical and contemporary literature that is being taught in most high school classrooms.

But the news is not all good. The multiple-choice portion of the writing test is brutal. According to the College Board, the test "measures students' ability to express ideas effectively in standard written English, to recognize faults in usage and structure, and to use language with sensitivity to meaning" (*SAT Program* 2000). Even after working through several practice tests, I found the errors that I was being asked to identify subtle and confusing. I know that I have not adequately prepared my students to face such questions. For years I have taught skills within the context of student writing, correcting sentences and discussing commonly made errors with the whole class. The weakness of this method is that many students never generate the kind of complex constructions the SAT requires them to analyze. This does not mean that we should return to a drill-and-worksheet approach to teaching English. But we do need to be more systematic and intentional about how we teach students the structure of their language.

Very few teenagers' speech patterns replicate standard written English. If students are not taught formal usage in school, there is little chance they will ever acquire it. The possibility that only those who can afford expensive test preparation tutorials will succeed on SAT tests troubles me a great deal. All students deserve to be prepared.

I tore open the envelope containing my results with considerable trepidation, my mind racing. What if I blew it? How could I face the students who took the exam with me? What possessed me to do this in the first place? Fortunately my worries were unfounded. I earned a perfect score (800) in writing and a 790 in literature. I knew I missed that question about iambic hexameters when I answered it.

What I learned from this somewhat traumatic experience was that I needed to be more explicit in my teaching of both writing and literature. For students to be able to demonstrate what they know on high-stakes tests, they need both instruction in the content that these exams cover and practice answering questions in such formats. I think we can accomplish this without distorting what we believe about authentic writing and response to literature. Choosing not to will only hurt the students most in need of our help.

Helping Students to Kick In Instead of Kick Back

Senior year is a heady time for twelfth graders. High on thoughts of college, prom, and graduation, many seniors forget that these last ten weeks of high school may be their last chance at getting the academic aid they need. Instead of taking advantage of the help teachers offer, they shrug it off. "I can pass with a D, right, Mrs. Jago?" Right, George.

As an example, let's take a set of papers I recently read from seventy senior students. I estimate that if these essays had been submitted for California or any other state's proposed exit exam, 20 percent to 30 percent of the students would fail. It is possible that knowing that high stakes were attached to the assignment would inspire better performance, but I'm not sure. The papers were full of rudimentary errors in mechanics, usage, and syntax—mistakes that in an ideal world would have been eliminated from students' writing by the sixth or certainly the eighth grade.

Who's to blame? While there is always room for improvement, I know how hard my colleagues in this district work.

Most of us have extremely high standards and expend an extraordinary amount of effort to ensure that students know what they should be doing when they put pen to paper or fingers to keyboard. As a result, many of our students write extremely well, with voice and flair and, on a good day, even a sense of organization. But others haven't a clue. Too many students have attended thirteen years of Santa Monica schools and still mistake *their* for *there* and spell so poorly that any thoughtful reader would shudder.

When these students enroll next fall at a community college or university, help will be available. I know of no more caring and knowledgeable professionals than the individuals who teach in remedial writing programs at these institutions. But the ugly truth is that the further behind a student is in English when he or she enters college, the less likely he or she is to graduate. How a student performs senior year is a strong predictor of future academic success or failure.

So what's to be done? The first thing we—parents, teachers, counselors, administrators, relatives, employers, friends— must do is disabuse seventeen-year-olds of the idea that senior year is for kicking back. The irony is that it is exactly those students who have not kicked in during their entire school career and as a result have the most catching up to do who are the first to complain when a senior-year teacher demands academically rigorous work.

The second thing we need to do is reduce class size. While I can push myself to correct seventy essays in a weekend, I can't possibly get around to help thirty-five students individually in a class period. I do my best to get to everyone, but unfortunately those who get the most individual attention are often the squeaky wheels who put in the least effort and are just calling me over to moan that they don't know what to write (when actually they hadn't bothered to listen to my instructions). With thirty-five students in a class, an enormous amount of my energy is spent simply keeping students on task and maintaining a civil learning environment.

It's possible that some students would be better served through an independent study program. As it is, those who refuse to get down to work in a traditional classroom setting interfere with the learning of others. Although schools take enormous pride in having low dropout rates, of equal importance is the quality of instruction. And when instruction is repeatedly interrupted by unruly behavior, learning suffers. Attendance does not equal an education.

I know that many of my seniors only come to school because (1) it's a place to meet their friends, and (2) their parents will kill them if they don't don a cap and gown come June. Undaunted by these circumstances, I still believe that it's my job to teach them something.

More and more states have begun posting "No Exit" signs on high school doors and refusing diplomas to students who cannot pass an exit exam. Although lawsuits will be filed on behalf of students who feel their education has not prepared them to take these tests, many students will be denied a diploma. As a teacher I know how many factors that are outside of my control contribute to a student's ability to pass an exit exam, but I must take responsibility for those I can control. Before students can get beyond standardized assessments, they are going to need to get through them. I believe a curriculum that inspires students to excellence is the only one that has the potential to make this happen.

Eight

Beyond Teaching Standards

*A*ccording to Delaine Eastin, California's state superintendent of public instruction, January 25, 2000, marked the beginning of a new era in educational accountability. On that date, 1999 Academic Performance Indexes (API) and rankings for the vast majority of public schools were made public. The goal of the Public Schools Accountability Act is to reward schools where students achieve academically and apply pressure to those where students do not. In order to ensure that schools are compared with others in like socioeconomic circumstances, complicated formulas have been applied to results from last year's standardized test scores. But most readers of the API rankings simply want to know two things: Who is Number One? How does my child's school measure up?

Ranking Schools Is Not the Same as Ranking Basketball Teams

The public's familiarity with sports rankings probably makes the use of such lists inevitable. When we read that Arizona's basketball team is ranked second and Stanford's third, or that USC is the best team in the Pacific Ten Conference, we have confidence that such placement on a scale is fair and relatively accurate. We take it for granted that straightforward game results determine rankings. Applying the same approach to academic achievement, we tend to forget that, while basketball results involve counting how many times a ball goes through a hoop, educational results are rather more complicated to measure.

Schools and teachers should be held accountable for improving instruction, and measuring every school's progress toward achieving academic excellence over time makes eminent sense. It doesn't make sense to assume that a test score is the best measure of such progress. Even when other indicators, such as attendance patterns and dropout rates, are factored into the equation, the matrix is still incomplete. How can you rate a teacher's enthusiasm for literature or instinctive ability to transmit that enthusiasm to students? How can you quantify the extent to which the culture of a high school campus either supports or undermines student achievement? Where are children's attitudes toward learning measured? Shouldn't schools receive progress points for helping parents become more involved in their children's education? What about measuring a reduction in the number of hours spent in front of the television on school nights? That would be true progress.

Basketball fans have likely started grumbling that similar factors—the quality of coaching, team morale, and a player's work ethic—are exactly what determine the number of times a ball goes through the hoop. There is one huge difference. Every college team in the rankings, whether first or last on the list, practices with regulation balls in a clean and well-lighted gymnasium, wearing first-rate equipment. In California's public schools no such parity exists. Until it does, we need to think long and hard about judging the quality of a school on the basis of its API ranking.

Merit Pay

Although teachers unions oppose salary plans that discriminate among teachers on the basis of performance, I believe that if this country wants to improve the status of its teachers, the surest path is through merit pay. In no other profession do the most accomplished practitioners receive only longevity raises.

Teachers who want or need to earn more must either leave the classroom for administration or leave the profession altogether. This is absurd. Gifted and talented teachers not only work harder and longer hours than their competent colleagues, they also inevitably take on many unpaid leadership roles at their schools and in the larger teaching community. It only makes good sense that these individuals should be rewarded. Merit pay will help to keep the best teachers teaching.

The problem with most merit pay schemes outlined by politicians and district administrators is their narrow definition of *merit*. Teachers should most certainly be judged on the basis of their students' achievement, but authentic student achievement involves a great deal more than improved test scores. The merit that a genuine merit pay system should reward is a complex combination of content knowledge, instructional skills, and connecting with kids. To suggest that the best evidence of these meritorious traits can be found in students' answers to multiple-choice questions is to make a mockery of a teacher's work.

For the sake of argument, let me compare two of my own classes. My period one class of thirty-five tenth graders has almost perfect attendance. They arrive on time with books in hand, homework completed. These students do almost everything I ask of them with minimal complaint and, if not maximum, always reasonable effort. My period five class of thirty-seven twelfth graders has about a 15 percent absentee rate. Many students stroll in late from lunch with anything but poetry on their minds. It often takes five minutes to collect their attention and get them focused on the lesson. Several will spend the entire period doing nothing. Last week I had to stop a group of seventeen-year-old, six-foot-tall boys from throwing Play-Doh at each other.

You might be thinking that I am going to tell you that the first group of students makes me look like Super Teacher and the second group makes me seem a barely competent instructor. In fact, I believe the opposite is the case. I know I am doing a good job with my period one class and have no doubt that most of them will score at the eightieth percentile or above on the Stanford 9 exam, but it is my work with the second group of students that best demonstrates my merit.

Every day is a constant battle to make my period five students put their minds to work. It takes everything I have ever learned about classroom management and everything I can think up fresh each day to engage them and keep them on task. I wish I could fill this page with the poems and essays these students have written in the past month. Their work demonstrates a level of excellence that many of these wild and crazy teenagers had no idea they were capable of. Because so many of them still make elementary mechanical errors, we work hard at revision. I insist that correctness counts. When a piece of writing is finally polished, students read it with pride to their classmates. Last week a poem of Sandy Mendez's drew a standing ovation.

Working with this particular group of students has been one of the most challenging experiences of my professional career. It has also been one of the most rewarding. Would test scores reflect the work I've done and the growth students have made? I don't think so, particularly when I would be held accountable for students who attend only three days a week as well as for those who sleep through class. A better measure of my "merit" might be to interview students asking them what they feel they have learned. A portfolio of students' writing might accompany a taped interview in which students comment on the lesson and their own process of following an assignment through to completion.

Such evaluation of a teacher's merit is obviously messy and inevitably a bit idiosyncratic—more like the work of an anthropologist than a psychometrician—but I just don't see how the real work of good teaching can be measured any other way. If you want to know which teachers deserve merit pay, ask the kids. A few students may give you names of teachers who were good pals to them or easy graders, but for the most part students know very well when they have had a great teacher. The evidence is in their work.

A Case of the Willies

How could an educator quibble with candidates who promise that, if they're elected, there will be a "fully qualified, well-trained teacher in every single classroom, everywhere in this nation, before the next four years is out"? Though I very much want to see this happen, Al Gore's campaign pledge gives me the willies.

One of the ways Gore plans to make good on his promise is through an $8 billion fund for scholarships, college aid, and signing bonuses for new teachers. On the surface, helping young people pay for their own education seems like a sound way to attract them to the teaching profession. Where the logic breaks down is that there is in fact no shortage of college graduates. Attracting talented young people to teaching is going to take more than financial incentives. It's going to take the declaration of a national emergency.

What gives me the willies about Gore's plan is that he touches upon all the issues voters seem to want to hear about—rigorous teacher certification exams, teacher evaluations based on student test scores, firing teachers who do not meet national standards—yet he offers no specifics. To begin with, there are no national standards for teachers. Nor is there a national curriculum against which to measure student performance. (I have always been partial to the idea of a national curriculum, but of course only if it matched what I believe should be taught.) In this country, education has always been a local affair. Instead of wasting his breath and taxpayer dollars on programs that will only ever provide token relief, a presidential candidate should use the bully pulpit to attract the best and the brightest to teaching.

In 1960, John F. Kennedy attracted the best and the brightest minds to Washington, D.C. The next president should inspire the finest, most creative minds in this country to imagine themselves in the classroom. Transitional, Peace Corps–like stints won't do. America's schools need teachers who are in it for the long haul. Gore has proposed a second $8 billion incentive plan that trades increased teacher pay for tougher teaching standards. I hear this and once again get the willies. If we attracted the best and the brightest to the profession, no one would have to worry about "getting tough" with teachers. Many of my colleagues are so demanding of themselves that they burn out rather than give in to any lowered standards in their classrooms. No wonder I've got a case of the willies.

It's a Wonderful Life

As politicians rack their brains to find incentives to entice talented individuals to choose to teach, they might consider reflecting on what a Nobel laureate in literature said about teaching. According to John Steinbeck,

> It is customary for adults to forget how hard and dull and long school is. The learning by memory of all the basic things one must know is the most incredible and unending effort. Learning to read is probably the most difficult and revolutionary thing that happens to the human brain and if you don't believe that, watch an illiterate adult try to do it. School is not easy and it is not for the most part very much fun, but then, if you are very lucky, you may find a teacher. Three real teachers in a lifetime is the very best of luck. I have come to believe that a great teacher is a great artist and that there are as few as there are any other great artists. Teaching might even be the greatest of the arts since the medium is the human mind and spirit. (Wallsten 1989, 234)

The job of teaching is not an easy sell. While starting salaries of twenty-five thousand dollars plus benefits may sound decent to a recent college graduate, the ceiling on teachers' pay does not. How many other outstanding professionals can look forward to making only sixty thousand dollars a year regardless of the quality of their performance? Many teenagers I know dream of driving sixty-thousand-dollar cars. On a teacher's salary, they would have no chance of achieving such vehicular status.

Of course most teachers choose the field for idealistic rather than economic reasons, and what keeps them going year after year is a love for kids and an unflagging dedication to helping students learn. But how many of these dedicated idealists are urging their own children to become teachers? Very few. Like other middle-class parents, teachers want their children have a better life, and whatever "a better life" means in a larger sense, it certainly includes financial security. I also think teachers are reluctant to urge their offspring to follow in their footsteps because they know too well that being a teacher simply doesn't garner much respect.

I worry that unless society's attitudes toward its teachers become more like Steinbeck's, many potential artists will never find their way to the classroom. Teaching is no longer the career of choice for smart young women intending to work for a few years before starting a family. Today most smart young women fully intend to work at a job throughout their lives. Few have any illusion that one income will be able to support a family in the style to which they aspire. The other problem is that telling friends at a college commencement you are heading for an elementary classroom just doesn't sound as thrilling as saying that you are moving in the direction of a court or operating room.

Along with financial incentives for the best and the brightest entering the profession, we need to figure out better ways of showing respect for the remarkable work many teachers do every day. More money would be nice, but professional working conditions are equally important. I also think that when experienced teachers at a school feel good about their jobs and themselves, the novice teacher down the hall can't help but notice. Many fledgling teachers are scared away from the profession by the litany of complaints they hear over the photocopier.

As tough as the working conditions may be, for anyone who loves the medium of the human mind and spirit, I can't imagine a better career choice than teaching. It truly is a wonderful life.

Works Cited

Addison, Joseph. 1712. *The Spectator*, no. 335 (25 March).

Beck, Isabel L., Margaret G. McKeown, Rebecca L. Hamilton & Linda Kucan. 1998. "Getting at the Meaning: How to Help Students Unpack Difficult Text." *American Educator* (Spring/Summer): 66–85.

California Department of Education. 1997. *English Language Arts Content Standards for California Public Schools.* Sacramento: California Department of Education.

Cazden, Courtney. 1998. *Classroom Discourse: The Language of Teaching and Learning.* Portsmouth, NH: Heinemann.

Csikszentmihalyi, Mihaly. 1990. *Flow: The Psychology of Optimal Experience.* New York: Harper & Row.

Cziko, Christine. 1998. "Reading Happens in Your Mind, Not in Your Mouth: Teaching and Learning 'Academic Literacy' in an Urban High School." *California English* 3, no. 4 (Summer): 6–7.

Darling-Hammond, Linda. 1997. *The Right to Learn: A Blueprint for Creating Schools That Work.* San Francisco: Jossey-Bass.

Delpit, Lisa. 1995. *Other People's Children.* New York: The New Press.

Dillard, Annie. 1987. *An American Childhood.* New York: Harper & Row.

Fisher, M. F. K. 1988. *Consider the Oyster.* San Francisco: North Point Press.

Gardner, John W. [1961] 1984. *Excellence: Can We Be Equal and Excellent Too?* New York: W. W. Norton & Company.

Jago, Carol. 1990. "Death Comes to the Term Paper, or the Extinction of Termapapersaurus Rex." *California English* 5, no. 3 (Spring): 13.

———. 1999. "The Term Paper Revisited." *English Journal* 89, no. 1 (September): 23–25.

———. 1999. *Nikki Giovanni in the Classroom: "The Same Ol' Danger but a Brand New Pleasure."* Urbana, IL: National Council of Teachers of English.

———. 2000. *With Rigor for All: Teaching the Classics to Contemporary Students.* Portland, ME: Calendar Islands.

———. 2000. *Alice Walker in the Classroom: "Living by the Word."* Urbana, IL: National Council of Teachers of English.

Kohn, Alfie. 1993. *Punished by Rewards.* New York: Houghton Mifflin.

Lamott, Anne. 1994. *Bird by Bird: Some Instructions on Writing and Life.* New York: Pantheon Books.

Massachusetts Department of Education. 1997. *Massachusetts English Language Arts Standards.* Malden: Massachusetts Department of Education.

Mather, Cotton. 1977. *Magnalia Christi Americana: Books I and II.* Edited by Kenneth B. Murdock. Cambridge: Harvard University Press.

Meier, Deborah. 1995. *The Power of Their Ideas.* Boston: Beacon Press.

Moon, Brian. 1999. *Literary Terms: A Practical Glossary.* Urbana, IL: National Council of Teachers of English.

National Council of Teachers of English and International Reading Association. 1996. *Standards for the English Language Arts.* Urbana, IL: NCTE.

Nea Today. 2000. Interview with Jonathan Kozol. "Kids Who Beat the Odds." *Nea Today* (April): 19.

New Jersey Department of Education. 1996. *New Jersey Core Curriculum Content Standards.* Trenton: New Jersey Department of Education.

Ohanian, Susan. 1999. *One Size Fits Few: The Folly of Educational Standards.* Portsmouth, NH: Heinemann.

Olson, Lyn. 1999. "In First Year of Tests, States Must Brace for Foul Weather." *Education Week* (23 February).

Pressley, M. & P. Afflerbach. 1995. *Verbal Protocols of Reading: The Nature of Constructively Responsive Reading.* Hillsdale, NJ: Erlbaum.

Radzinskii, Edvard. 1997. *Stalin.* New York: Anchor.

SAT Program. 2000. Princeton, NJ: The College Board.

Schoenback, Ruth, Cynthia Greenleaf, Christine Cziko & Lori Hurwitz. 1999. *Reading for Understanding: A Guide to Improving Reading in Middle and High School Classrooms.* San Francisco: Jossey-Bass.

Schwartz, Lynne Sharon. 1996. *Ruined by Reading.* Boston: Beacon Press.

Strunk Jr., William, E. B. White, Charles Osgood & Roger Angell. 2000. *The Elements of Style.* New York: Allyn & Bacon.

Wallsten, Robert, editor. E. Wallsten Steinbeck & John Steinbeck. 1989. *Steinbeck: A Life in Letters.* New York: Penguin USA.